REAL LIFE
SUPER HEROES

REAL LIFE SUPER HEROES

NADIA FEZZANI

DUNDURN
TORONTO

Cover image: Phoenix Jones. Photo by Peter Tangen.
Printer: Webcom

Library and Archives Canada Cataloguing in Publication

Fezzani, Nadia, 1976-, author
        Real life super heroes / Nadia Fezzani.

Issued in print and electronic formats.
ISBN 978-1-4597-3915-4 (softcover).--ISBN 978-1-4597-3916-1 (PDF).--
ISBN 978-1-4597-3917-8 (EPUB)

        1. Crime prevention--United States--Citizen participation.
2. Vigilantes--United States. 3. Community activists--United States.
4. Neighborhood watch programs--United States. 5. Heroes--United
States. I. Title.

HV7432.F49 2017   364.4'30973   C2017-903663-7
                                              C2017-903664-5

1 2 3 4 5   21 20 19 18 17

We acknowledge the support of the **Canada Council for the Arts**, which last year invested $153 million to bring the arts to Canadians throughout the country, and the **Ontario Arts Council** for our publishing program. We also acknowledge the financial support of the **Government of Ontario**, through the **Ontario Book Publishing Tax Credit** and the **Ontario Media Development Corporation**, and the **Government of Canada**.

Nous remercions le **Conseil des arts du Canada** de son soutien. L'an dernier, le Conseil a investi 153 millions de dollars pour mettre de l'art dans la vie des Canadiennes et des Canadiens de tout le pays.

Care has been taken to trace the ownership of copyright material used in this book. The author and the publisher welcome any information enabling them to rectify any references or credits in subsequent editions.
                                              — *J. Kirk Howard, President*

The publisher is not responsible for websites or their content unless they are owned by the publisher.

Printed and bound in Canada.

VISIT US AT

 dundurn.com | @dundurnpress | dundurnpress | dundurnpress

Dundurn
3 Church Street, Suite 500
Toronto, Ontario, Canada
M5E 1M2

To my love, my inspiration, my light.
Thank you for your unconditional support.

CONTENTS

INTRODUCTION

I have been told that even the police don't often venture into some of Seattle's tougher neighbourhoods in the early hours of the morning. On most nights it's as if law enforcement has surrendered this part of the city to the junkies, pushers, pimps, and gangsters. I would have been terrified had I been there alone, but I knew I was in safe hands. I had local legend Phoenix Jones and his crew of Real Life Super Heroes watching my back. I felt as though I was in a scene from *Watchmen* as I walked the dangerous streets with Jones and company. They, much like fictional superheroes, wore elaborate costumes and bulletproof vests. Phoenix Jones's distinct black-and-gold protective costume, inspired by Nightwing — Robin's subsequent identity — was known nationally by the time I met him, and his teammates all wore equally decorative protective gear. As something of an embedded journalist, Jones insisted I look the part and the team contributed to my look: a red mask and black protective equipment suitable for a Real Life Super Hero.

I had been warned that anything could happen in these dark, nearly lawless streets. I couldn't tell if people were staring at us because we looked like easy marks — perhaps easy-to-mug yuppies who had gotten lost on the way to a costume party — or because of our costumes. Being so conspicuous felt unnerving at first. Later on I learned that trouble often seemed to find Phoenix Jones, and this night would be no exception. A hooded man was following us. He had a gun in his hand, and yet I wasn't afraid. In any other situation I probably would have run away, screaming for help. Instead, I felt powerful and ready to confront the gunman. Maybe it was the costume I was wearing. According to at least one study,[*] people wearing costumes can feel more confident. My bulletproof vest was protecting my vital organs. I figured that the chances of getting shot in the head or an artery were slim; we were moving, and so was he. *Hit me anywhere else and I'll cope with it*, I thought. I was willing to face the pain. The sudden rush of adrenalin made me almost feel invincible. I had no fear. I finally understood the incredible high of what it's like to be a Real Life Super Hero — willing to risk my life for the good of others.

In the heat of the moment I was ready to confront the man. But in the end I didn't have to. One of the guys had called the police, and the gunman fled once he saw law enforcement arriving on the scene. Now looking back, I find my surge of bravado foolhardy. I could have been shot in the leg or arm. A bullet could have hit an artery and killed me in mere minutes. Bulletproof vests are no guarantee of safety.

When the adrenalin wore off and I had some time to think, I started to analyze why these people risk so much. What motivates a person to dress up and go looking for danger? Were they uniquely brave? Probably not. After all, many occupations require physical courage. Police officers, firefighters, soldiers, and even paramedics put themselves in harm's way for strangers all the time. Were they "crazy" people? Maybe. But I felt that there was much more to RLSHs than individual eccentricity.

⚡

---

* Jonathan O'Callaghan, "You Are What You Dress: Clothing Has a Significant Effect on Self-Esteem and Confidence, Claims Expert," *Daily Mail*, May 30, 2014, www.dailymail.co.uk/sciencetech/article-2644076/You-DRESS-Clothing-significant-effect-self-esteem-confidence-claims-expert.html.

Before embedding myself with Real Life Super Heroes, I spent years interviewing, researching, and writing a book about serial killers. In hindsight, I realized that superheroes and serial killers share a number of similarities — at least in terms of their psychological and sociological histories. As with serial killers, there are several types of Real Life Super Heroes. Many serial killers seek power and control over their victims. Similarly, many of the Real Life Super Heroes fighting crime on the streets are people who have been disempowered, through either their own victimization or their feelings of powerlessness in the face of issues like sexual abuse, crime, addiction, and homelessness. Both serial killers and RLSHs usually have impactful events from their past that will later define their extreme behaviour. Both kinds of people feel an intense need to take control to make themselves feel more powerful or secure. However, while serial murderers want to decide their victims' fates and take lives, RLSHs want to *save* lives and keep people from harm. Ultimately, their attempt to save others is, in many cases, an attempt to save themselves. To the RLSHs, even if they are killed or grievously injured, at least they have lived for something and had a purpose. After hearing about Phoenix Jones, I knew I had to learn more about these costumed crusaders.

1
MY FIRST
SUPERHEROES

A good friend of mine initially piqued my interest in Real Life Super Heroes. He told me about a news story he was watching. Some guy in a mask and Batman-like costume was making headlines by running around Seattle fighting crime. My friend explained that "Phoenix Jones" had been involved in a skirmish with a man who'd been beating on some other guy. Jones, the news said, was a mixed martial arts expert. He had intervened and was attempting to hold the attacker down in a headlock after calling 9-1-1. Before the authorities arrived, however, one of the assailant's friends showed up and forced Jones at gunpoint to release the attacker. When Jones complied, the man he'd been holding kicked him in the face, breaking his nose. The story made the rounds of the national news. Even *Saturday Night Live* picked up on it and mocked Jones. But I was intrigued. Having spent the previous four years researching and writing a book about serial killers, I thought that maybe I'd stumbled onto a more positive story. I began research to see what else I could learn.

⚡

It wasn't easy entering the world of Real Life Super Heroes. People who wear masks usually do so because they don't want to be identified. It's not like guys like Phoenix Jones have publicly listed phone numbers! I did manage to find an email address supposedly belonging to Jones, or PJ as people have come to call him. But my inquiries went unanswered. Other than what had been on the news and what little I could find online, I had nothing.

Well, not entirely nothing. In the course of my research I learned that there was a whole subculture of these Real Life Super Heroes. I came across a guy calling himself "Thanatos," the personification of death. He was operating out of Vancouver, Canada. Unlike Jones, Thanatos didn't "fight crime" per se, but spent his time doing outreach with Vancouver's large homeless population. I didn't quite understand at the time how his mission fit in with what Phoenix Jones was doing, but I was at least getting somewhere with this elusive community. Maybe it was his Canadian politeness coming through, but Thanatos actually answered my email and even agreed to participate in an email interview. In the course of our correspondence, I asked him if he happened to know how to get in touch with Phoenix Jones. I was somewhat surprised when he told me that he did but only indirectly. According to Thanatos, my best bet was to contact a man called Peter Tangen, a successful Hollywood photographer and unofficial PR man for a whole group of Real Life Super Heroes. Tangen was like a promoter/gatekeeper for some of the more prominent members of the RLSH community.

Reaching Tangen was a challenge. My emails went unanswered for days and then weeks. All I wanted was an interview with Seattle's most famous superhero! I was about to get more persistent when Peter finally got back to me over the phone: "Nadia, I have an amazing opportunity for you. Something we have never done before."

It turned out that "something" was a telephone conference call with five of the most notable RLSHs. I was especially fortunate because Jones, to this point, had refused all but in-person interviews. For once, he would make an exception.

⚡

It was already midnight as I waited by the phone and went over my interview questions one last time. Peter Tangen had arranged to have Phoenix Jones, Geist, Nyx, Phantom Zero, and DC's Guardian on the line. The group represented a wide range of superhero styles. Jones was the crime fighter; Geist lends assistance to people who are in distress or suffering through natural disasters; Nyx was a former crime fighter who gave it up to focus on homeless outreach with her boyfriend Phantom Zero; and DC's Guardian took it upon himself to teach people about their rights and responsibilities as citizens.

I dialed in to the conference number a few minutes early. The New Yorkers, Phantom Zero and Nyx, were already on the call. According to the pictures I had seen, Phantom Zero had one of the darkest and most frightening of the superhero costumes. He wears a black cape over his broad 6'4" frame. A white skull-like mask disguises his upper face, and black makeup hides the rest. A white shirt and red tie accent his attire. In short, not the kind of guy you'd want to run into in a dark alley if you didn't know that he was a "good guy"!

I made small talk with Phantom Zero while we waited for the other participants to join the call. Since many of them had not spoken with each other in a long time and some of them had never even met, I gave them a few minutes to talk among themselves. Listening to them provided an interesting glimpse into their world. Rather than serious topics like crime fighting, I heard them chatting excitedly with one another and laughing. New introductions were punctuated with, "I've heard about you when you did …" or "Do you remember the day …?" After a few minutes, I welcomed them officially, thanked them for joining and started the interview.*

"First of all," I asked, "what are your duties as superheroes?"

DC's Guardian answered first: "It's my responsibility to protect people's rights and privileges that this nation offers by teaching it to future generations. I strive to help the helpless and to educate people."

During his military service, DC had had many different experiences. He now works for the government and travels domestically and internationally. As a superhero, he often stands on the streets, sharing pocket-sized

---

* The interview is shortened for the purpose of the book.

copies of the United States's founding documents, such as the Constitution and the Bill of Rights. Some people mock him without understanding his motivation. DC's Guardian is one of the rare colourful superheroes. Most of them only wear one colour, black, but he proudly wears the red, white, and blue of his country.

Geist is probably the one with the most unique style. He projects an image that is more like a western-style hero with a noir flair. He wears a long duster-style trench coat. A green bandana covers his face while his sunglasses hide his eyes. A cowboy hat tops his outfit.

"I fight for the forgotten," Geist says. "I defend and protect people who are overlooked by society, who slipped through the cracks. It could even be animals who are neglected in pet shelters and are in danger of being euthanized. It could be the environment. You know, the problems that we all just kind of gloss over as we go about our daily lives."

Nyx was the next to speak: "My main goal is to help the helpless. Most of us have seen some undesirable things in our lives where people are suffering in one respect or another. That just prompted me to try to prevent further suffering. That was pretty much instilled in me at a young age. I realized that I could take a proactive stance on that and actually do something meaningful."

Nyx, unlike most heroes, doesn't hide her face. She also does not have a specific uniform, but dresses in many different ways. In her most popular picture, she's wearing an alluring black and red outfit: a black fishnet shirt revealing a red bra. A crimson sheer scarf only slightly obscures her face below the eyes, and she leaves her beautiful long brown hair loose. She is also one of the few female superheroes who patrolled alone despite the inherent risk.

Phantom Zero contributed to the discussion next. "I pledged to myself to make a difference. I want to stress free thought. In the end, there is a very important message behind it. Personally, I want people to ask questions and find their own truth, their own personal journey. I want them to learn about what is important to them and to achieve it."

"And how do you achieve that?" I asked.

He explained that he patrolled to find people in distress. He helps many of them to write and express their often-difficult emotions. He also does homeless outreach, donates to community centres, and encourages people to do good deeds around themselves.

Speaking a mile a minute, Phoenix Jones plunged in. "You'll see a lot of the average person walking around who sees stuff but does nothing. I thought that was pretty cold. I have years of martial arts experience, a couple years of bodybuilding, and I am a certified nursing assistant. So I know how to deal with trauma and troublemakers. My criminal father taught me how criminals think. So I search for people and look for criminal activities. Make lots of sacrifice. I literally just neglect things because I'm out doing the things that I do. It's borderline obsessive, and when I see something that is a crime and I know that I can stop it, it's very hard to persuade me otherwise, as DC has found out. We've been on patrol where DC had to talk me down from stopping crime."

Indeed, several of the superheroes work together. They travel far and wide to meet and collaborate, and it can be expensive and time-consuming. But they say that as they work together, relationships are developed and their efforts are amplified through collaboration.

"I'm not going to say it's everyone's message," added Phantom Zero, "but superheroes are not a mythology. They are ideals and virtues. They are a manifestation of people pretty much empowering themselves. So I feel a part of a community when we do this. It's something that we do, it means a lot to us, and it's very symbolic."

"You are framing yourself as the epitome of superheroes," said Geist. "I mean … how crazy, weird, and insane is that? Just think about DC's suit; he's wearing the American flag! I think we all try to be the best we could possibly be once we put on that suit."

That last comment resonated with me. At least they realized it might seem a little crazy to some people. Thankfully, when talking to them, I could tell they were not delusional. They genuinely seemed like they just wanted to do good.

"But why do you hide your identity?" I asked.

Geist talked about protection. "If I'm doing my job correctly, then I am getting some particular people ticked off at me. I really don't need a visit from gangs, such as the Latin Kings, the Bloods, the Crips, MS-13, and I do hope I'm making them angry, dissatisfied, and aware that they don't belong in my city."

The Real Life Super Heroes are just like Spider-Man, Batman, Iron Man, Superman, and any other superheroes we're familiar with. Their loved ones can become a point of vulnerability. Superman's Lois Lane gets kidnapped. Spider-Man's Aunt May is targeted by villains. Many fictional superheroes find their loved ones threatened and sometimes even killed.

A superhero's career can also be at risk. The common explanation is a fear of losing their jobs if their bosses find out what they do outside of work. After all, if someone can be fired for what they put on their own personal Facebook page, what would a boss think about superheroism as a hobby?

Geist later revealed to me that he and I share a similar occupation — he works for a daily newspaper. Does that sound like a certain Man of Steel from the comic book world? It was extremely important to Geist to keep the fact that he was a RLSH from everyone in his professional life. He recounted a time when his editor assigned him to cover a story on the local Real Life Super Hero Geist. He said it felt surreal to be told to write a story on his secret alter ego. It put him in an awkward position and, with a desire to remain ethical, he thought it best to tell his editor all about his secret life. It remained between Geist and a couple of co-workers for years until he eventually switched jobs.

DC mentioned that he covers up to hide his skin; he doesn't want people to attach a skin tone or ethnicity to his persona.

On the other hand, some people do not need to hide. As mentioned previously, Nyx, for example, doesn't cover her face anymore when she's doing charity work. Her task is not as risky as those fighting criminals. "Back home in Kansas," she said, "I did hide it. I didn't really want my identity known or for my family to know what I was doing. Now in NYC, I have a little more freedom in that regard."

Phantom Zero also only hides his face on occasion. "When I began originally, I assembled this persona, this image and appearance, and I didn't really know what I was going to do with it or where I was going with it. A lot of people love superheroes, but a lot of people also hate Real Life Super Heroes, and I know that some people have actually sought out RLSHs, sought out their identities, tried to cause them harm. So, since most of what I do is for charity and homeless outreach, I really don't do it to protect myself from the public, but mostly to protect myself from people who might harm me; whether it is people at my job or people trying to find out information about me, find out where I work, people who might harass me."

"But," I asked, "unless you're a criminal, why would you want to harm Real Life Super Heroes? Wouldn't you want someone to protect you when you need it?"

"I just think there are certain people who are malicious for whatever reason," said Phantom Zero. "Celebrities have stalkers. Real Life Super Heroes have people that are angry at us because what we are doing is something that is not necessarily seen as positive or good. I think that people don't take the time to look at what we are actually doing. I think they just look at the costume. And I know a number of Real Life Super Heroes who actually have been harassed or bothered by individuals."

I could never have imagined how far the threats could go. Aside from verbal harassment, some people went the extra mile to make superheroes' lives miserable. These "trolls" have done unthinkable things to hurt Real Life Super Heroes.

As I learned more about their work, I felt like I was peeling an onion. This community had more layers than I had anticipated going into my investigation.

DC's Guardian added, "In today's environment, there is so much going on, no matter what part of the world you're in, that a lot of people become blinded by walking down the street. When people in costume step out on the road to help out a stranger, be it a homeless individual or the victim of a crime, people's heads turn and it opens their eyes to what's going on in their neighbourhoods. Some people tend to have issues with that light being shined in their own eyes because they may be the ones walking past them every day and not lifting a finger to help. For others, it's because they're not trying to make any investment — not even a little bit each day."

It was Phoenix Jones's turn to answer. Since the 22-year-old fights crime, his situation was a little different. Much like Batman, he breaks up fights, gets into them when he has to, and sometimes calls the police, thus occasionally contributing to someone's incarceration. That is more than enough to make enemies.

Jones explained that he started his work as an unmasked civilian. Since he doesn't drink, he would drive his adopted brother and friends to and from the bars for a couple of bucks.

"I would see people doing crazy stuff," recalled Jones. "I'd also spend half of the money on food and things for the homeless. If I'd see a bar fight, I'd stop it. It got to the point where I couldn't live a normal life because people were starting to get mad at me. They'd say something like, 'Hey! You broke up that bar fight last week. You got my cousin arrested!' and it got weird. Then I had my son and I figured I've got to quit this. It wasn't until another incident that I changed my mind. I then *had* to do this, but in a safer way for everyone. Personally, I would love to take my mask off and be on the cover of every magazine that wants to do an interview with me. But because I value and I love my family so much, I have to wear the mask. The weird thing is that the mask is actually way more famous than the guy underneath the mask. People love me with the mask on and I've had the same guys saying terribly mean things to me with the mask off."

⚡

Having their identity revealed is only one of the risks involved. Not surprisingly then, many RLSHs carry weapons. Geist and DC often travel for patrols, and they have to be well informed and aware of local laws, state by state.

Geist once had some of his expensive equipment seized at the airport. His suit weighs between 30 and 40 pounds because of what he carries. His typical gear includes a stun baton, a metal baton, pepper spray, various other weapons, and even marbles to throw on the ground in case he needs to delay pursuers. Although Phoenix Jones also travels sometimes, it's mainly for interviews. In Seattle, he and his group carry extendable batons, tasers, stun guns, sticks, different types of pepper spray, a stab-proof vest, and — like most RLSHs — a bulletproof vest.

But not everyone carries as much equipment. For example, DC only carries the basics, such as a camera. "I rely mostly on my training and things that I can find locally, depending on what type of situation I'm in. I prefer not to carry weapons per se because it doesn't matter how good you are, there's always a possibility that it can be taken away from you and suddenly the situation gets worse." Phantom Zero does not carry weapons either. And things for Nyx have been different since she left Kansas, where she would carry an extendable baton and mace. Since she moved to New

York City, she brings only a camera and a cellphone since laws for carrying weapons in New York are strict.

Nyx actually moved to New York to be with Phantom Zero two years ago.

"We met through the Real Life Super Hero community," added her boyfriend. "She was originally in Kansas and I was in New Jersey. We eventually decided to meet each other." Today, they both work for the same IT company and patrol on weekends.

Although most superheroes do not include their loved ones in their masked crusades, there are a few couples within the community, from crime fighters to activists. Phoenix Jones and his fiancée, Purple Reign, are among them, though he would have never been able to persuade his ex-girlfriend to do the same.

"I had a pretty hard time convincing my son's mother about what I was doing," declared Jones. "My suit was really expensive."

I wondered how expensive and inquired. I was shocked at the response: $5,500! Jones had to ask his mother to co-sign on a credit line to get it, but he told her it was for a car. Most superheroes start their costumes with very basic clothing and build their gear up over time, just like Spider-Man. Nyx doesn't really have a specific costume, and Phantom Zero just used what he had at home and made a mask. DC and Geist designed and co-designed their costumes. Phoenix Jones started with very basic clothing and finally paid to get gear made by a specialized manufacturer.

Phoenix continued: "I got my military buddy to help me buy this military gear, and I was assembling it and obviously trying not to tell anyone. I didn't want to tell my girlfriend until I did something that I figured was heroic. I put my gear in a closet ... I don't know why I didn't think she was going to look in that closet. She opened it and the bulletproof vest fell out and all these weird pieces of equipment. She didn't say anything and just put it away. Then she turned, looked at me, and said, 'I don't want to know!' No more than three weeks later, she clipped a newspaper article and put it in our room. The headline was of a masked man who stopped a fight in a bar. She looked at me and goes, 'You're done. Over!'" Phoenix and others on the call laughed heartily at this.

But things have changed since then. Purple Reign takes part in PJ's activities and even started her own fundraising campaign to help victims of domestic abuse. Both PJ and Purple were then part of the Rain City

Superhero Movement. There are more than eight other people on the team, but Purple is the only woman.

"I started the Rain City Superhero Movement because I felt that I was not accepted by the RLSH community," explains PJ. "I mean, the people who did not accept me are not the true voices of Real Life Super Heroes. Everyone on this call here are real heroes. They've all done real work. They are all out in the streets doing real patrols, doing real organizations, giving out real food and helping real people. And they don't care what you look like. They don't care if you're black. They don't care if you're purple. They don't care if you have five toes on your hand as long as your heart's in the right place, and that's what makes this group of people real heroes. Whereas the people who were talking about me badly, who had a very strong opinion about the RCSM, are not a good representation of the group. Everyone has their own perspectives and their opinions. Some people, for example, support our activities and some people are neutral, others may not like what we do. I'm sure there are people who love me and hate me, and there are people who love Geist and hate Geist."

Indeed, not everyone likes Phoenix Jones. Resentment toward him might be greater than for any other superhero. Some people don't agree with his tactics. Some people hate him to the point of making it their job to put him down and ruin his reputation. The hatred is palpable. One rival superhero even had a picture of Jones on his punching bag. There seemed to be more than a little bit of jealousy and rivalry within the superhero community.

In some instances a RLSH will publicly back Phoenix Jones, and others in the community will stop talking to them. I read numerous Facebook posts along the lines of "if you're friends with Phoenix Jones, unfriend me." Geist knows. It happened to him. Many in the community say that they don't approve of Jones's behaviour; therefore, others shouldn't talk to him.

Geist explained, "We are a very diverse group and we represent this very idea. Being a Real Life Super Hero doesn't mean we are all members of the same club. It's more like a descriptor or a heading of the idea we are all a part of."

Real Life Super Heroes have existed for over 40 years. Some consider the Fox to be the first one. He alone fought against the polluters of a river, starting his mission in 1969.

"We're all trying to do something good," said Geist, "and it's good to have friends. Actually, some of my favourite experiences are meeting Real Life Super Heroes for the first time, shaking their hands, looking in their eyes and going, 'You know, I might be crazy, but if I am, you are, too!' [Laughter] 'And you know, you've got a friend right there!' We believe in the same crazy things."

As Geist continued to talk, he hesitated, apparently distracted by someone in need of help. "Sorry about that. The first thing I do when I go to help someone is I look down at my belt to look for my utility kit, and then I realize, 'Oh no! I don't have my suit on!' [Laughter] Then I'm like, 'Okay, well … I don't need a suit!'"

We all laughed and several people thanked him for "sharing that mindset."

⚡

A brief lull in my questioning brought out some spontaneous insights on the shared mindset as the superheroes spoke among themselves.

"I know the real identity of Phantom Zero," said PJ, teasingly.

"We know so much about Phoenix and his name that we have blanked it out of our memory," joked Geist. More seriously, "I once accidentally learned the name of a Real Life Super Hero by seeing his ID. I felt terrible about it! I showed him mine. When we find out stuff like that, we try to forget it. It's none of my business."

"When we did the photo shoot with Peter [Tangen], down in LA," recalled DC, "Everybody met at the hotel, and I was in a corner booth, in my suit, doing what I was trained to do as a superhero. Then I spent half the evening watching the others in another corner having a good time. It was interesting and really nice to see. But I never introduced myself, because as DC, I try to keep my true identity and name out of the picture."

"And that's one thing about DC," recalled PJ, "during that event, he never unveiled himself at all. I did because I thought, 'Well, okay … I'm among friends, far away.' I got to take off my mask, my hat, everything. DC was covered all day and went in solitude to eat. No one saw him. But the first time I went to see Peter, I was in California to take some photos with him. I didn't know him that well, we had talked on the phone, but I had never met him in person. When I got there, it was late. I didn't have time to get a hotel room, so I crashed at his house. I took my ski mask upstairs and slept on the ground. When I woke up in the morning, I had my mask on, some boxers, and a white T-shirt. Peter was like, 'Are you kidding right now?' And he laughed."

⚡

I was glad they felt comfortable enough to recall stories that showed just how seriously they took the security of their alter egos. For whatever else you could say about them, they sure seemed to have a lot of fun. But things then got a little more serious.

"I actually have a secret story about Geist," said Phantom Zero. "I was going to be kicked out of the place where I was living. I hadn't known him for very long and very casually talked to him on the phone. I was concerned because I didn't know what to do, while being on the verge of homelessness. Not even knowing me, he offered to wire me cash, which is one of the nicest things that anyone has ever done for me. Luckily, by the end of the weekend, I was able to find an apartment and I wasn't a transient, which is great because I know how bad it can be out there. So that was a very nice thing he did and it's not something that he publicizes."

"I don't think I ever did that," said Geist.

"Yes you did. You said you would wire me cash," repeated Phantom Zero.

Everybody laughed. Someone quickly said, "He didn't say that because worms will come out of the woodwork and start asking him for money!"

⚡

Our conference call had started at midnight and it was now closing in on 2 a.m. I wanted to end the meeting on a high note, so I asked them each to tell me about times where they'd enjoyed some success.

"Children's Hospital," answered DC's Guardian. "I was visiting this one child and not realizing how bad it was with his treatments. He was refusing to accept his medicine. I apparently said something to him and he was there holding my finger. He took the medicine and I had no idea that it was hurting him, but we continued on with the rest of the day and they let us take a picture together. When I'd gotten back to Arizona, I was contacted by one of the nurses who told me his whole story. He had vicious forms of cancer. He was not accepting his medicine and it was really causing concerns in the hospital; without mentally accepting it, the body was not accepting it. So apparently, what I had told him was, 'I am going to give you some of my strength.' And when he got the picture back, he would carry it to all of his chemotherapy treatments and all of his appointments. When he got scared, he told the doctors, 'It's okay. DC gave me some of his strength.' I think I got more out of the visit than he did, by realizing that something that might seem so insignificant can mean so much to somebody else."

As a journalist, I try to remain a neutral observer, but I had to tell DC how inspiring and touching that story was.

Geist answered next: "There were some floods in South Eastern Minnesota in 2007," he said. "It didn't so much affect my own city as it did a lot of cities east of Rochester. I knew what the floods could do, so I brought a truckload of supplies. The day after the flood, I hit St. Charles, Minnesota, and dropped off some goods. Then I went to Lewiston and dropped off some more. A pastor there told me, 'Lewiston doesn't need as much supplies as the next town. The people in Stockton got hit hard. They have nothing.' As I drove into Stockton, the bluffs were crumbling. I could see mudslides and rockfalls were happening or that they had happened. The roads were barely passable. I got in the valley and the town was caked with mud. There were homes that were gone and several fatalities. I found the emergency centre and it was busy. People needed supplies. The Salvation Army was there with a truck of supplies. I was also there, in full costume. I got out of the truck with a couple of bags and I saw a security agent on foot. He was passing in front of me and I said, 'Sir, sir.' He turned around, looked at me and immediately put his hand on his taser. Then he looked me up and down and paused. I said, 'Where can I put these supplies?' He said, 'Ahhh! Right over here.' And I said, 'Okay great, because I have a truckload more.' He asked, 'Do you want help?' And I said, 'No sir! I'm a superhero.' And he laughed. I think it was the first laugh he had all day."

Phantom Zero didn't have such stories to tell, but not necessarily be-cause he is without success. "I have small stories, mostly about individual people who I have helped through minor crises. I have a bunch of those stories, but they are not mine to freely tell because they deal with people's personal pain and particular details of their lives."

Nyx talked about giving money she got from an interview to a shelter for women and children fleeing abuse, up in Rochester, New York. She told me that her mother was disabled and deaf, and a survivor of abuse. Her mother's experience made this a cause near to Nyx's heart. I could tell it was an emotionally charged topic for her, and once more I found myself marvelling at how life experiences shape lives.

PJ also wanted to support a cause and like many of the others, was influenced by his tough upbringing. "What I thought was my greatest failure was probably one of my greatest successes," he said. "It was back before I was really known. I used to run around in spandex pants and a blue spandex shirt, a fedora hat, and a bulletproof vest. I would literally jump out [of] alleyways, bushes, and other random places to bust up a fight, and then run back into the bushes. It was really exhausting and really ineffective. But I was walking in this alleyway when all of a sudden, I'm on my back and I can't breathe. I'm looking up into the sky and I feel like I'm gonna die! I rolled up under a dumpster and I just kind of laid there, holding my chest. I was thinking, 'That's it! I'm dead!' I looked down to see that someone had shot my bulletproof vest, and it was burning my hand. I looked around and I did not see anyone around me except for the people behind me, like 150 feet away, in a bar. I started to call 9-1-1, then I realized I couldn't do that, because I was supposed to be a superhero — not being out here getting shot by a phantom menace! So I picked myself up crying, and I took all of my stuff off and went into the emergency room in my underwear. That must have been one of my biggest failures. I'm supposed to be out there fighting crime! It wasn't until later that I was talking to someone who knew a lot of people who hung out at the bar. He said. 'You know, you were down there, in bulletproof gear, trying to keep things safe. Someone fired a gun and out of all the people it could have hit, it hit you. The only guy within the vicinity who happened to have a bulletproof vest on.' I consider that to be a success."

Although the bullet didn't go through the vest, it left an important bruise. I was surprised he was willing to expose so much vulnerability, especially in front of other superheroes. He admitted to being afraid and to crying. I respected him for not trying to play the indestructible tough guy.

⚡

As the interview was wrapping up, I asked, "Do you have a message for people?"

DC said, "I normally tell people that everybody is either one of two things; they are either a good example or a bad example. It's up to them to decide which one they are, but at the end of the day, their actions often speak louder than their words. The group of people that you have on this phone call are all good examples."

Geist answered, "It is time for everyone to step up, to be responsible for other people besides themselves."

"I grew up with disabled parents," said Nyx, "I would like to see more of an air of equality, more understanding between everyone regardless of if you look or seem different in any way. We are all just people, and we all want to be happy and fruitful, and we should all just try to help other people. So that's what I would really like to see."

Phantom Zero's motives are very similar to DC's. "People are individuals," said Phantom Zero. "They have the ability to make their own choices and the ability to live their lives the way they want to live their lives, and express themselves however they want to express themselves. Essentially, I want people to realize the greatest thing we have is our ability to choose. Our independence and our individual natures make us strong. I want people to just be people and not part of a collective mentality. Just be yourself."

Phoenix Jones followed with, "Mine is kind of harsh. I don't want to be perceived as rude or rash, but my thought is 'Get over yourself!' Get out in the world and do something. If there is a crime in your neighbourhood, call 9-1-1. If a father assaults his family, get on it. If people are being bullied, then stop the bullying. A lot of people just whine and I'm tired of it. Shut up and do something!"

⚡

It was the end of the interview, at least for most of the group. I thanked them once again and waited until everyone hung up the phone — except Phoenix Jones. As he was the only one of my interviewees who fights crime, and since this was the subject I was most intrigued by, I wanted to ask him some questions on a one-on-one basis.

I asked him what made him want to become a superhero.

PJ described the day it all began for him: "We were at a water park called Wild Waves. I had left my phone in the car, so we were running back to grab it. Someone had broken a window on my car. My son had tripped over the glass and cut himself pretty bad. I picked him up and he was shooting blood out of his leg. There was a bunch of people around and I yelled at a guy who had a phone, 'Call 9-1-1!' He goes, 'I can't.' I asked, 'Why?' He said, 'because it would ruin my YouTube clip.' He had been recording the whole thing on his phone and he would not help! Eventually, I got my car unlocked and I called the paramedics myself and got my son taken care of. There were people who had seen the break-in and were all, 'Yeah, it was a tall white dude. He broke into your car.' No one called the cops. No one did anything. And because of the negligence, my son was injured. He now has a scar on his leg for the rest of his life. As I was cleaning my car, I found a ski mask with a rock in it. The thieves must have been slamming the glass with this. I left the mask in my car and I called the police again. I said, 'I have the mask, if you want to DNA it or something.' The police basically laughed at me and said they don't investigate car break-ins. They said they get too many. They didn't care. It just made me mad."

I could only imagine his frustration. Phoenix continued, recalling taking the mask, cleaning it up, and putting it in his glovebox. He talked about being part of a breakdancing team. When he was at a club for that activity, he left his phone in his car because everything in his pockets would have fallen out while he was dancing. One day, he was going back to his car to get something when a guy asked him if it was his friend outside who needed help.

"My friend's face was flopped open and was just gushing blood. I asked, 'What happened?' They were like, 'Dude, that guy hit him with a stick!' And he was standing there, laughing with his friends. There were about 70 people outside the club. I ran to my car, and I could not have planned this any better. It was dark outside. I opened the glove box and the little light went on. This light shined and this mask was sitting there. I had already been a comic book fan and seeing it, I thought, 'If anyone is going to be a superhero, it's me!' I threw the mask on. I had a hat that my friends had used to dress up like the Blues Brothers. I threw it on and I just felt like this moment of justice was about to happen. I was just fresh off of a cage victory, I was in amazing shape, and I walked up to this guy and he just took off. I chased him, I tackled him, and I hit him a few times. I took the stick and I was going to whoop his ass when the police rolled up on me."

Luckily for PJ, since his friend didn't accuse the assailant, the assailant didn't accuse PJ. PJ recalled that the authorities were nice to him and very helpful. He then talked about a photo someone took of PJ and a police officer on the scene. I went online to find it. It was interesting to see his costume development since that time. In the photograph he is dressed the way he previously described: a black fedora with a white band, the black ski mask found in his car, a tight black shirt that showed his muscled upper body, and a white belt. His first superhero team dressed the same, except they all had blue shirts.

We went back to talking about past events, and I asked about rumours I had heard. He either agreed or denied and explained. Then we talked about other, more personal things and finished the interview at 3 a.m. Phoenix offered to be available in the future, an offer that, as it turned out, I would take him up on very soon.

⚡

I was very thankful that he had given me so much time, especially for someone who only does interviews face-to-face and who is in high demand. But instead of satisfying my curiosity, these hours of conversation only made me more curious about Real Life Super Heroes. They had become more real and genuine to me.

Now, I wanted to know more about the superheroes and meet with them. I needed to see for myself what type of people they were, in real life. So I decided to accept Peter's invitation to meet with masked crusaders from all over the country in New York City, during the fifth annual Superheroes Anonymous event. As Peter explained, this was my chance to meet the very individuals I was interested in writing about, and to introduce myself and my project. I received some pointed advice from multiple superheroes whom I told about my trip. They all said the same thing: "If you go to NYC, do *not* mention that you want to visit Phoenix Jones."

2

SUPERHEROES ANONYMOUS

I had no idea what type of people I was going to meet at the Superheroes Anonymous event, held yearly in New York City. But I was going to meet Real Life Super Heroes, people who, masked and equipped, dedicate their lives to help and protect others. No superpowers, you might say? Well, plenty of comic-book superheroes lacked superpowers. Just look at Batman and Iron Man, for example. Actually, without the ridiculous side of the fictional personas, the Real Life Super Heroes reminded me of the 2010 movie *Kick-Ass*, in which "real" people dressed up at night and fought crime.

I hoped I would not be meeting a bunch of delusional misfits. I preferred that they be rather normal people, wanting to give back to society for one reason or another. If it appeared to be too insane, I could always leave. One thing was for sure: I wasn't going to miss out on the opportunity.

Although this topic seemed to be something new in the world, some of today's superheroes have practised their vocation for more than 20 years.

Public awareness, on the other hand, increased in 2011 when HBO aired a documentary on them, *Superheroes*.

I felt, however, that the documentary deliberately made these people look like pitiable weirdos. It depicted Mr. Xtreme living in a messy apartment and losing a fighting competition; the New York Initiative having violent members; Dark Guardian having a hard time clearing drug dealers out of public parks. It also portrayed Super Hero as less than super and little more than a flashy car and a costume, and showed the Salt Lake City Black Monday Society in outfits that frightened people.

But my experience so far had shown me that there was a human side and even something admirable in what they were doing. I wondered if the film had cast them in an unflattering light through editing, or if its depiction was true to reality.

⚡

Since I had been told that superheroes from all over the country usually attended the Superheroes Anonymous event, I was really looking forward to meeting with Thanatos and Phoenix Jones in person. Unfortunately, because of the large amount of snow that fell that weekend, most superheroes outside New York City had to cancel their attendance. Instead of lasting three days as in years past, the activities of Superheroes Anonymous were only going to be held on Sunday. I still decided to go.

The next day, around noon, I entered a slightly rundown brick building. It didn't seem like the right place. When I got inside, the large space was nearly devoid of people. A few tables covered with orange fabric lined the wall near the entrance. I stood surveying the room when I was approached by a young man.

He introduced himself as Life. With the help of a friend, Life had planned the entire event. He struck me as a very intelligent and well-educated fellow. As a superhero he originally wanted to fight crime. But when he couldn't find any in his area, he decided to be more of an inspiration and aid to homeless people instead. As he changed his focus to helping the transient, he realized that none of them remembered him after having met him. That's when the idea of a costume occurred to him. And it seemed to work. People remembered him more easily. He doesn't hide his face much, just a black half-mask that covers the contour of his eyes. The rest of his outfit is black jeans, black tie, black suit vest, a black fedora, black fingerless gloves, and a white collared shirt.

A few people arrived while I chatted with Life. I joined them at the centre table where yards of various fabrics were laid out, along with white masks, glue, buttons, and a sewing machine.

"You have to make your costume," a young woman told me. Me? Although I wasn't really into it, I thought I'd better get into the super-hero spirit!

More and more people showed up. Everyone was excited about making their superhero persona. Some had long coloured capes; others were covered in leather. Chatting with a few people, I found that they were all excited about the good deeds they were about to do.

The entire time I was there, a TV crew was filming for a Discovery 3D documentary. I had requested not to be in the film since I was doing media work as well. A young and vibrant journalist from California was also there to cover the event. Later on, a researcher showed up to feel the vibe for another potential documentary.

After working on our costumes, it was now time to learn self-defence from a martial arts trainer with over a decade of experience, superhero Dark Guardian. He is featured in the HBO documentary confronting drug dealers in a park. On this day he was going to teach a few self-defence manoeuvres to about 20 people.

When Dark Guardian was done with his lesson, everyone cleaned up the tables and it was time for a serious talk. We gathered the chairs together and sat down quietly to focus our attention on Life as he explained our next task: homeless outreach.

⚡

There were probably about 30 people in the room listening to Life's address. Behind him, on the wall, was the black-and-white logo of Superheroes Anonymous; it looked like a logo version of the speaker.

"You don't approach homeless people just any way you want," he said. The first two rows were filled with attentive adults. You could have heard a pin drop.

Life explained that many homeless people get bullied, harassed, and beaten by strangers, so he stressed the importance of approaching homeless people courteously. He shared many of the best practices he and others had learned about doing homeless outreach: always introduce yourself, show you want to do good, and ask them if they need something specific. Verify that they're not allergic to something you're about to give them, and check if they have a health condition that could be affected (diabetes, for example). Ask if they already have what you are offering (winter coat, socks, blankets). Another good thing to know is that the most requested things are toothbrushes and toothpaste. Socks, too. And it's important to travel in groups when doing homeless outreach. Although many of them are good people, they are just human: some are nice, and some might not be.

After learning more about the mandate, the superheroes prepared for their mission. Volunteers had laid out supplies for care packages on the tables. The items had been collected and donated by people from all over the world directly to RLSHs. There were piles of plastic bags, snack bars, toothbrushes, toothpaste, soap, socks, clothing, coats, and blankets — and chocolate. As Life said, "It's also good to give them a little something extra." We filled our bags, trying to put a piece of everything we had in them.

It was important to separate men's clothing from women's, and to not forget that many women are also homeless. As Life mentioned, these women are often forgotten. Why not make bags with sanitary products for them?

With the training complete and the care packages assembled, it was now time for patrol. We got ready to go, dividing the group into two. I was placed with Dark Guardian and Dusk Citizen — a slim, helmeted man clad in blue motorcycle leather — and about six other people. The camera crew followed us. Since another woman, Erin, and I were not thrilled about being on camera, we stayed back and got acquainted. Erin was attending the event for the first time. Being from New York City, she was looking to scope out a charity and see if she could raise corporate sponsorship for the superheroes. Unfortunately, since RLSHs act on their own, they would not be the right candidates for her corporate helpers. But she found the event inspiring and wanted to stay. When I asked her why, she responded, "Their hearts are in the right place. They just want to help people and they do it the best way they know how and sometimes that means doing things others would deem as 'unsafe.'"

Our group encountered homeless people who were either alone or with a friend or two, often leaning against a brick wall or finding refuge in a building's doorway. Some of them seemed happy to talk with new people, especially the older ones. The first thing most of them asked us was if we had toothbrushes. We didn't have enough for everyone, but no matter what, the recipients were extremely grateful for whatever we could offer.

A few of them impressed me. One was asked if he wanted a blanket. He politely declined, saying he had what he needed, and asked us if we could make the same offer to someone who was close by who needed one. He could have easily kept the blanket and traded it.

We came across a fit black man with a clean haircut, clean-shaved, well-dressed, and well-spoken. Had he not said he was homeless and been hanging out where he was, it would have never crossed my mind that he might be in need of help. He said he was actively looking for work.

Eventually we ran out of people to help on the street. It was probably just too cold and too late. We stopped by a shelter, where we gave everything we had left to the receptionist. We saw many men in there and a few women. I wondered what it would be like for a homeless woman to live among all of those men.

⚡

The experience was enlightening. It was nice to speak with the homeless, get a new perspective, and share that experience with new friends. Just as Life said, we learned by talking to the people on the streets that many of them had lost everything and were trying to get back on track. Although some people may have nothing because of drugs or other addictions, such as gambling, most of them are on the streets because of difficult childhoods, living through rough situations, such as sexual abuse or domestic violence, or having drug users, alcoholic, or even homeless parents. Others have had difficulties building a normal life after having been in care, in the Armed Forces, or in prison.

Not all homeless people are alike. Some have mental health issues that prevent them from keeping stable jobs. Others have been impoverished from the high cost of medical bills in the United States. Entire families have become homeless as a result of the economic crash of 2008, while up to half of homeless women and children are victims of domestic violence. Also, not all homeless people are unemployed. Some have jobs, but the cost of housing in some cities has vastly outstripped the wages of many working-poor people. Many young people in foster care leave the system as soon as they turn 18 and become homeless as a result.

When considering the diverse causes of homelessness, I thought about Red Light. The petite young woman patrols the dark streets to help those in need by talking down a dispute or finding rides for those who are too drunk to drive. She serves as an extra set of eyes and ears and calls authorities when she witnesses suspicious activities or mistreatment of animals.

Red Light worked toward her EMT certification after trying to rescue a man suffering from a heroin overdose. As part of her employment, she receives routine training on awareness and threat-response tactics and weapons handling, and briefings on local gangs and Homeland Security threats. She also participated in optional courses on wilderness survival and self-defence.

Growing up, she was subject to sexual abuse and domestic violence. She was also diagnosed with a malignant tumour in her stomach at 28 years of age. It took her five years to get the necessary funds to go through her operation.

"Every day is another chance to make things better. Life is only as bad as you let it be. It's easy to forget how much we have when it feels like we have to fight so hard to keep it. It hasn't stopped me from being kind to people. I still patrol. I still help others. Anyone can do something. Anyone."

I was impressed by her courage, kindness, and positive outlook, so the fact that she was homeless hit me hard. She works full-time, but because of her hospital bills and the high cost of living, she lives in her car.

But there is hope. According to GoodWorks, by the time a person is living on the street, they have already exhausted their interpersonal resources. This contributes significantly to loneliness and despair. A simple offer of friendship can sometimes make the difference in initiating their recovery.

The patrol ended. It was time to go back to the event space.

*

I had an important meeting to attend. I was going to meet with Zero, one of the four creators of the New York Initiative. As I understood it, if he said yes to my book project, many others would follow. Dressed in all black, Zero was sitting on one of the orange couches talking with people. I went over and introduced myself.

Zero was smiling. We walked toward the entrance to isolate ourselves from the crowd and the loud music. Standing up, he was a few inches taller than me, making him about 6'2" or more.

He had already told me he wasn't big on media interactions, as he doesn't like people talking about him, but he was willing to give me a chance to tell him about my idea.

I was told that, like many other superheroes, Zero had a rough childhood. While we were talking about the past and the present, he shared some of his personal philosophy, and it stuck in my mind. "Some people live in the past," he began. "But what happened yesterday was yesterday. Today is a new day. Stop carrying the past with you. You have all the opportunities now," he said, with a slightly gravelly voice.

We ended the conversation with a handshake, and I moved on to join Erin and meet with other superheroes. During the evening, we had a lot of fun with Shade, also from the New York Initiative. Shade was a very nice man and quite attentive. For the first time, he was debating whether or not he should reveal his identity tonight by taking off the black mask that matched his protective gear. He said he had never shown his face before in public as a superhero. Later on, he decided it was the time for him. When he showed us his true identity, we discovered a young black man in his early twenties, with a lovely smile.

*

I'd gone to this meeting of superheroes unsure of what to expect. I'd seen the HBO documentary that made many doubt the sanity of some RLSHs. What I'd discovered instead was a community of well-meaning people determined to make a positive impact. Many of them had skeletons in their closets. Many had had their own brushes with early-life traumas. I didn't see anything laughable so far, but I couldn't stop thinking about the motivation. What was really driving these people?

I would learn about many more positive aspects of the community, but negative elements were also about to be revealed.

3

THE ONLINE COMMUNITY

I am a police-sanctioned crime fighter, crime preventer, and Neighborhood Watch block captain, who has been publicly lauded by my local police department ... for doing a good job at what I do. I have decided to remove and de-friend any ass-hats that have, for whatever reason, decided to diss, dishonor, or otherwise screw up the public image of the RLSH movement.... I'm tired of the fucking *Kick-Ass* wannabes, and will expose them for the imbeciles they are, in the fullness of time, with extreme and most satisfying prejudice.

—The Eye

After the release of the HBO documentary, RLSHs became more and more popular on Facebook. Those who did not already have a profile made one. The number of new superhero profiles seemed to surge overnight.

On the positive side, it showed that many people wanted to do more for their communities and causes. But the problem might be that it seemed too easy. By the time I started writing this book, I had close to 500 Real Life Super Hero friends online. A few months later, I had friend requests from about 100 more. But how many were real? Probably no more than 50. Were the others just a bunch of marginalized, lonely people, desperate to belong? Could that be what was driving this movement?

Soon after my visit in New York, the news reported that two 17-year-old boys and one 18-year-old wanted to punish pedophiles. They set up profiles of underage girls and chatted online with men. They filmed a few meetings with potential pedophiles and put them on YouTube. Two of them were dressed as the Flash and Batman. The boys taunted and humiliated the suspected perpetrator in a public place. The YouTube videos were soon taken down by authorities.

The RLSH community was mad. Although they thought the boys' intentions could be seen as good, the RLSHs did not generally accept their actions as positive. The consensus was that the boys were too young and improperly trained to do that kind of thing.

There are very few superheroes under the age of 18. Those who are typically help adult superheroes with their missions or help the homeless until they come of age. Others in the RLSH community, however, wondered if the criticism of the predator vigilantes was born of jealousy.

As if this wasn't enough of a schism, additional news followed and stirred up the community even more. Phoenix Jones was having an extremely polarizing effect on the community when he made the headlines…. again! The latest Phoenix Jones incident seemed to be tearing the online superhero community in half.

One superhero wrote on Facebook:

> PJ, go fuck yourself. The title says it all. You can claim I am jealous, you can claim that you are the best, and no one will ever compare to your greatness. I am sickened by your sight, your ill representation of the hero you claim to be. All those who were exalted always fell, as will you…. You are a fraud, a self-righteous wannabe. Pray I never make it to Seattle, because I personally will take you down.

I checked out the Facebook profile of Dark Guardian, with whom I had patrolled at the Superheroes Anonymous event. He weighed in on the PJ controversy:

> This is not a damn comic book. This is real life with real consequences. Acting, hamming it up, playing up things for the camera is pathetic and dangerous. This is not fantasy; this is people's lives. More and more I want to leave behind all this and just do this without any contact or association with others.

The replies went on and on. Everyone had an opinion about PJ.

> PJ is no model, and he is certainly not part of this community. What PJ did was utterly dumb and he deserves every bit of what he got for his rash behaviour, but everyone threatening to leave because of the bad rep following him, that's just unnecessary. What should be done, is everyone unfriend Phoenix Jones, and be done with his existence. He can't affect us if we don't associate ourselves with him and his actions.

> Obviously anyone who sides with PJ on this whole "spectacle" is nothing more than a poser who thinks that they'll win over a false model.

Some more neutral comments:

> I've been a vocal critic of PJ in the past. But he seemed to be taking steps to improve his interaction with other people, to document his claims about crime: fighting, etc. So I've been growing more favorable toward him ...

> I think PJ needs time to grow like any of us.... All of us do things that make us questionable as far as being up for the job. What matters is that we continue to work to be better and support each other as brothers ... even when we don't agree.

It went on and on. Some people were on Jones's side. And those who defended him were blocked on Facebook by other superheroes who were against the Seattle superhero.

I had to find out what exactly happened, but the articles were contradictory. One claimed that Jones started running toward men who were fighting and pepper-sprayed them to separate them. Another one said that these people were just having fun and dancing when Jones ran in their direction and sprayed them. Although I didn't really know PJ, the second story was hard to believe. But PJ had a cameraman with him, Ryan McNamee, as well as a journalist. McNamee posted the video on YouTube. The video showed PJ and his teammates involved in complete chaos. Pepper spray was flying, people were shoving and yelling, a woman at one point began hitting Jones with her shoe. At another point a vehicle, presumably driven by one of the people involved in the fight, peeled out and struck a pedestrian. It took the police at least 24 minutes to arrive on the scene.

Jones was arrested on the spot. And for the first time, a journalist released his name — his real name — Benjamin Fodor. The online reaction was a flurry. People researched his pictures, posting and sharing older photos of him from when he was an MMA fighter. PJ's identity was now known and he was everywhere on the news.

Right away, I called the *Journal de Montreal* and the *Metro* newspaper. I was ready to write an article about it. The *Journal de Montreal* called me back first, and I was right on it. I called Peter, and he promised me an interview with PJ. Many in the media had requested to speak with him, so I was grateful. Once Jones had been released and was waiting to appear in front of a judge, I reached him by phone and asked him a series of questions:

> Nadia Fezzani (NF): Phoenix, will you continue to fight crimes, now that your identity has been revealed?
> Phoenix Jones (PJ): Certainly. At this point, too many people believe in what I do. Many people are inspired. I know that I have an impact in my region and I shall not stop.
> NF: Is what you do legal?

PJ: Absolutely legal! We have a long history of patrol. We are not different from the Guardian Angels.

PJ explained that the police are often called after a crime is committed, and although he knows he cannot be everywhere, he wants to patrol and try to intervene during a crime or before a crime occurs. That said, he would like to have a better relationship with the authorities. But for people who would think of starting patrolling the streets like Phoenix does, he does not recommend it.

PJ: This kind of work is not for everybody. There are many sacrifices to be made and you must be very well-prepared. But for those who really want to, you have to have equipment at your full height, including a bulletproof vest. You must know what you can use legally in your city, as means of defence. It's necessary to have insurance and a good lawyer.

NF: Speaking of danger, are you mad at the police for revealing your name?

PJ: Yes. It is a really bad move from them. They made it so that I stop fighting crime. It puts my family in danger. I am waiting for an apology from them.

NF: Do you have a plan for your safety?

PJ: Yes, I have a good idea of what I am going to do.

A few days after his arrest and release on $3,800 bail, the judge decided to drop the charges. In court Jones was asked to take off his mask. When he emerged from court, masked again, over a dozen radio reporters, journalists, and TV crews from all over the world awaited him. Since the police had kept his gear, PJ was dressed in his old black and bronze suit and mask.

Standing in the middle of the media frenzy, the 23-year-old removed his mask from the bottom, lifting it on top of his head. Camera flashes came from all angles, and he said, "I'm Phoenix Jones. I'm also Ben Fodor. I'm a father. I'm also a brother. I'm just like everyone else. The only difference is, I decided to make a difference and stop crime in my neighbourhood and my area."

The online community was divided. Some said he did his best while others put him down.

PJ was all but ostracized from the online RLSH community. And as if the loss of support and the heavy criticism weren't enough, Phoenix Jones, a.k.a. Ben Fodor, lost even more than his secrecy because of that night. After having worked with autistic children for five years, accompanying them in their activities, teaching them about life, playing with them, and being a counsellor, Ben Fodor lost his job. The Department of Social and Health Services took away his licence and said he was no longer allowed to work with disabled or autistic children.

4

SUPERVILLAINS

Whﬁle immersing myself in the online community of RLSHs, I met a man calling himself Lord Malignance. He is what is referred to as a supervillain. Nothing really surprised me at this point. After all, what's Batman without the Joker? Superman without Lex Luthor? I guessed even RLSHs needed their foils.

The "villains" typically wear creepy masks and costumes, but I came to learn that they play an important role in the Real Life Super Hero ecosystem. I heard all kinds of rumours about supervillains that seemed to range from plausible to absurd. I was told that certain villains were drug dealers, hackers, or stalkers — people who wanted to deal out real trouble for Real Life Super Heroes.

I suddenly experienced a feeling of anxiety as I prepared to reach out to some of the villains. Somehow it didn't feel safe. I was somewhat surprised by my own hesitation, wondering, *Can they be worse than serial killers?* Actually, they could. The serial killers I had interviewed were safely behind bars. Supervillains hid their identities and were free. Free to do as they pleased. But they were the ones who could tell me about RLSHs without reservations. Of course, I felt more secure since communication could be established through chat and emails. But that was before I found out about how far some people could go to get attention.

⚡

I searched for the supervillains who appeared most often in Facebook discussions, commenting on and criticizing the actions of costumed crusaders. I approached them by introducing myself and my book project, asking if I could interview them about the community and their role in it. I mentioned I was looking for superheroes to interview and made it clear that I wanted to get in touch with those who set a good example.

I received a message from a villain named Lord Malignance. His look reminded me of Doctor Zoidberg from *Futurama*, with his white lab coat and three long cylinders that start from his glasses and go down to his chin. Lord Malignance's mask is gold, with his eyes hidden by large sunglasses and his head covered with black fabric.

Lord Malignance was in his third year in the community. He built an entire fictional headquarters, including a set he uses as a backdrop for his video communications. His goal is to inspire critical thinking through absurdity and imagination. When not criticizing superheroes, he often writes posts about fighting ninjas and building robots.

As we conversed, I understood that his message was only intended for the online superhero community. He then listed the heroes he believed in. "[The] heroes One has tested and found worthy — they believe truly in what they say. And One does test heroes. They are challenged in what they say, how they act, and how they respond to hostile ("evil") discourse — both civil/diplomatic and confrontational."

Lord Malignance is suspicious of the selflessness of superheroes helping people. "The capricious and random self-serving pantomime the superheroes perform is not justice. It is not charity. It is an attempt of the desperate to elevate themselves ("super") above citizens.... Stroking their own egos, and pursuing personal fame, by using citizens in need as props to their fake sacrifice is shameful. Consider: if superheroes didn't dress outlandishly, post, film, or promote their actions to as wide an audience as they can, they wouldn't be superheroes. They would be citizens. But would they do anything without seeking fame at the expense of the needy? They would not. They claim their purpose is to help, but they do nothing without the compensation of fame.

"As to my plans, One has been clear and persistent in my pursuit of my objective. The elimination of all Real Life Super Heroes. Every single one of them. This will be done by using truth. That's all. That's all that's necessary. Superheroes are trapped in a group self-delusion of their own making. Whenever the truth appears, they run from it.

"Like Kryptonite."

Lord Malignance listed some superheroes I should avoid and invited me to contact him again if I had more questions.

⚡

After more research online I found an interview with a self-proclaimed supervillain called JCreeper, a man who hides beneath a jester hat and a mask with a devilish smile.* When he was asked what it meant to be a Real Life Super Villain, he explained, "For the most part, we are the 'conscience' of the RLSHs. Basically we make sure the heroes don't cross that line into villainy. If you're doing a good job, protecting people and not being an ass for it, then fine. But once you step out of line (like the recent events with Phoenix Jones, for example), we will call you out on it and make sure people see the BS for what it is."

When asked if the world needed more villains, he made it clear: "Yes and no. The world needs more villains with a purpose and not more villains who just want to be thugs and criminals. Because that's not what we are about."

I asked JCreeper to give me names of superheroes to avoid as well. He had a couple more to offer than the previous supervillain, but the same names came back, with explanations.

When I started my research on the RLSVs, they were becoming known as the "Internal Affairs" for the RLSH community. They would regulate and ridicule those who called themselves superheroes but who

---

* "Interview With Real Live Super Villain JCreeper," by Michael Wilkerson, Blastzone Online, October 14, 2011, https://blastzoneonline.wordpress. com/2011/10/14/interview-with-real-live-super-villain-jcreeper/.

were less than heroic in their behaviour. Since some "heroes" pretended to be what they were not, these served as fodder for the villains, who loved to expose fakes. In this way, they contributed to a self-sustaining culture on the Internet. I also discovered that many villains simply wanted to hang out and play the same game as the heroes, without having to put in the effort.

Another motivation for some villains was the desire to mock what they see as the absurdity of RLSH, by exposing the implausibility of being either a villain or hero. Although some villains are hated by heroes, the majority of the RLSHs have come to recognize the value and balance the villains brought to the online world.

In a conversation about supervillains, Zero, from the New York Initiative, wrote on Facebook:

> Everything has an antithesis. I like that they exist. They've helped this community progress, believe it or not. And this is the reason I've thrown in with them a few times.
>
> They're just people calling out people with obvious delusions. Look past the titles and you can see it clearly. They don't claim lofty ideals, therefore they aren't obligated to follow them.
>
> They're really immune to mudslinging. They're an antibody to the current pitiful state of the community.
>
> They're not going to save the world ... but they may end up shaming a couple psychos into quitting before they hurt someone.
>
> Maybe. Worth their virtually harmless Internet existence.

Indeed, I thought it was important for superheroes to have some people to watch them. The villains practically became the moral centre of the community, ensuring that any hero whose actions threatened the reputation of the entire community would be held accountable.

For example, when Phoenix Jones used the pepper spray in a way that some considered too reactionary, the RLSVs made sure to spread the news everywhere to discourage the crusaders from doing the same.

Master Legend of Orlando has been seen, including in the HBO documentary, drinking alcohol while on a costumed patrol. In his case, the villains ridiculed him for his apparent alcoholism.

Zyklon B, a supervillain from the prominent group ROACH, the Ruthless Organization Against Citizen Heroes, took on a controversial name to match his approach to his criticism of the RLSH community. He uses inflammatory comments that are designed to straddle the line of propriety, especially with new or unproven RLSHs. Zyklon B helped bring to light an incident involving a superhero couple who became embroiled in an Internet sex scandal. They had allegedly allowed minors to view their homemade webcam videos. "The bad guys are really the good guys. And the heroes are the villains," says Zyklon B.

He explained to me his vision: "I believe that the SVs are needed in order to keep the RLSHs a little more honest. There are those out there who do not do the right thing and set a bad example for children and teenagers — I am strongly opposed to this. If you are going to take on the title of a "superhero" then you have a responsibility not only for yourself, but for how you are viewed in the eyes of the public. I want to see positive role models from this movement — not people who behave like a bunch of fools or seek media attention over doing what is right or moral.

"My goals have somewhat changed. I do not attack everyone who calls themselves a superhero ... just the ones who deserve it. There are those out there who I believe are genuine in what they are trying to do and truly wish to help people. I generally leave those people alone — and have actually become friends with some of them. It goes back to one of the most familiar quotes in comic book history (from Spider-Man): 'With great power comes great responsibility.' Influence over people *is* power — and to those that don't treat that power with the respect that it deserves — they will come in contact with the supervillains. My main goal is to make sure that the heroes stay heroic. And if I have to be seen as a villain for doing that — then so be it. Because in the end, I ultimately become the good guy.

"I will be honest: the costume makes things a lot more fun and theatrical for both sides. I mean, who wants to fight a 'hero' or 'villain' in a T-shirt and blue jeans? Come on — they get to wear costumes, then so do we!"

On the other hand, the established superheroes — those who have proven their ability and credibility — often love the villains, because they ensure the smooth running of the network. As some of them kept bringing up levels of villainy, I followed Zyklon B's advice and went to his group's website where the categories were explained:

> Class One Real Life Supervillain: Your persona is steeped in time-honored villain trope standbys like death rays and world domination, there is no time left in your day to bother with so-called "real life super heroes." They simply do not factor into your Blog, YouTube channel, Facebook page, Twitter feed, Podcast, Tumblr, and your still-in-its-planning-stages reality show where participants get fed to alligators. It's not about real life super heroes, it's about you and your endlessly amusing exploits to rule the world.
>
> Class Two Real Life Supervillain: World domination isn't enough to keep you occupied, and so you've looked into this "real life super hero" phenomenon and agreed that yes, every villain needs a hero. Laser-guided sharks and skull-shaped tropical hideaways are still your bread and butter for blog content, but every once in a while you feel the need to comment on the antics of vigilantes in spandex — perhaps you've even set up a formal agreement with an RLSH to "arch" them, because they, too, realize that there's plenty of fun to be had in crazy schemes that involve zombie piranha. At no point would you ever expose an RLSH's name or identity, to do such a thing would be uncomfortably like vigilantism itself.
>
> Class Three Real Life Supervillain: The trappings of fictional villainy are still in place — you routinely brag about how far your army of cyborg mutant apes have come since you began feeding them nanobots along with their monkey chow — but this is finely balanced with a

passionate distaste for what is happening in reality with costumed vigilantes, some of whom you've decided are very, very bad people indeed. You would never expose a real life super hero to harm, even the really rotten ones, but you've taken up arms online. Many of your posts have to do with shaming these vigilantes or haranguing them back into whatever hole they crawled out of. You have tracked down alter egos, just in case they think they can hide behind their mask if and when they lose touch with reality and do something terrible in the name of "justice."

Class Four Real Life Supervillain: Talking about mutant minions and other Sci-Fi supervillain staples has taken a back seat to the politics of getting real life super heroes to stop doing whatever they're doing in their entirety. You have tracked down the alter egos of all "heroes" you despise and you've made it a priority to expose their unseemly behavior and — perhaps — even expose their names and other details about their lives to the wider public. While you've committed no crimes, the term "legal gray area" has cropped up more than once. You would never ever do someone bodily harm, but you are very much on the edge of being completely obsessed with the RLSH.

Class Five Real Life Supervillain: Your stated goal is to beat a real life super hero up, with or without weapons, and possibly even kill them. You may have never even heard the term "Metavillain"; you heard about real life super heroes and now you felt that it is time to live out your Batman/Joker fantasies. Stop. When you jump out of the dark corner and bring your wrath out on a 45-year-old man with Asperger's syndrome who just donated plasma in a poorly made spandex costume, you will quickly learn that the Federal Prison System is nothing like Arkham Asylum, and reporters on TV compare you more to Jared Loughner than they do Two-Face.

Most supervillains I have chatted with are considered class three — Metavillains. They are not criminals. They are nice people. They just want to contribute, to make sure the superhero community does right by their title. However, in one or two cases, I know for a fact that I had been in contact with *real* villains ...

⚡

Tamerlane, who considers himself a class four, or four and a half, has a striking appearance. He uses his bald head and his imposing stature to his advantage. He is often seen with sunglasses and gold teeth. To add to his intimidating appearance, he also wears a black armoured glove that goes all the way up to his shoulder. His persona seems to represent a dictator or a rebel militia general.

He told me, "I have had my share of felony charges.... I desire no more! You can put 'class five' on my gravestone." Tamerlane is different than most of the others. I asked him to talk more about himself, and he recalled his early years at school. "My kindergarten teacher, Ms. Burns, would frequently bully me, pull my ears, and call me names. It was here I learned to mistrust. I also punched my first nose and kissed my first girl. It was a rocky start, but I was off and running. Throughout my childhood I desired to be James Bond or Superman. Life plays cruel tricks, and I was more akin to Blofeld and Lex Luthor than the heroes of the stories. But it was not until the 21st century that I should myself be revealed. One evening while watching the evening news I came across the story of Phoenix Jones and the Guardian, I believe the other's name was, and I said to myself: 'What arrogance! How dare they say they are Real Life Super Heroes! If they be heroes, then I shall be a Real Life Super Villain!' It is written on the grave of the great Asian steppe lord Timue Leng ... 'when I rise again, the world will shake.' I am he. It is of no coincidence that both the Occupy movement and the Arab Spring before that occurred shortly after my ... rebirth.

"I have been evil all my life, dear.... [That's] what makes Tamerlane different from the other supervillains. I mean it. Make no mistake. This is no cosplayer you see before you. This is a man with a mission. I walk the walk, meaning my acts of evil are performed daily and not just on a screen. I speak softly and carry a big stick as it were."

Of all the supervillains I had communicated with, he was probably the one I was the most careful with. After all, like they say in the community, "he seems legit!" But it was hard to believe the superheroes would agree with his extreme rhetoric.

I appreciated the help he was willing to provide, but I wasn't sure about meeting him in person, alone. *I would definitely need a superhero with me*, I thought.

⚡

The villains I chatted with were very straightforward about everything, whether it was about heroes or other villains. In contrast, many heroes seemed to censor their discussion of others for the sake of the movement.

I received a message from Malvado, a supervillain who covers his face with a mask made of thick black tape. He wrote: "The first thing I would have to say is that I am more than just a villain, I am a supporter and even a member of the RLSHs myself. I am a villain simply to police and question those the RLSHs will not do so themselves. I want to see these people succeed, as this is indeed a beautiful thing; people helping other people, those people motivating others to do the same, it's a really wonderful movement. I started out as just a villain, but not long after, their deeds inspired me to do the same. Now I volunteer three times a week at the local food bank.

"That being said, the villain portion comes in as a more aggressive way to defend this movement by singling out those that may be a danger to themselves or others or even those who are simply just bad for the community all together. The liars, those that manipulate for their own gain, the ones just looking to hurt people, these are the kinds of RLSHs that the RLSVs are always on the lookout for.

"I believe in doing good and passing on the faith in humanity and goodwill to others, but that doesn't mean I'm still not monitoring the RLSHs I encounter in my strange, often awkward adventure through the super 'hero' community. Either way, I'm a villain in spirit first and a RLSH in flesh second.

"The idea of the RLSV is not simply just to play villain to the RLSH's 'heroes,' but to do our part to preserve it for future generations. To keep it pure enough that it can survive all the social and political criticisms they face out there in the real world. Sometimes people are accepting and sometimes they aren't, but these things don't matter when there are people society ignores, some alone in their lives and others sleeping on the streets cold, but they are warm in their hearts knowing that there is someone looking out for them and at the end of the day, *that* is the only thing that matters. Aside from the Baroness, who raised money for a foundation on a specific day, I was not aware that certain villains also helped society."

As we were exchanging messages about a superhero, he suddenly stopped communicating. I waited for his answer for a little while and finally left my desk. I came back once in a while to check on him. Sometime later, he replied: "Sorry, I just had the police show up at my door saying someone told them that I might be a threat to myself and others. This has happened before to other villains, supporters of the RLSH [community] or RLSHs themselves sending police to peoples' houses to intimidate them. This is how much people hate me for criticizing them."

And then he moved on to talk about the superhero community again.

Wait … what? "Calling the police on you?" I asked. "How did they know who you are and where you live?"

"There is a guy out there who really has it out for me. He has associates that go around digging information out of people and apparently that's how he got my name. It baffles me that people take this so seriously."

That guy would have gotten his address in the white pages. He's not a hero; he's not a villain — just someone there to make trouble … a troll. I was asking myself what was the point of that. The answer would make itself known in due time.

⚡

As I was pondering, I wondered if I should contact more villains. Since the more people you know, the better, I decided to approach the Roaming Eye of Doom, a group that seemed popular in the RLSH community. They were a comedic group of metavillains led by Octavius Fong, an evil puppet made of fabric, with a blue nose. The Eye has had several members, such as Kaptain Blackheart, the Baroness, the Golden Don,

Professor Plague, and others. Their goal was to hold a "funhouse mirror" to the RLSH community by producing humorous videos, webcast radio programming, and online personas. The Baroness has also exposed false RLSHs whose goal was to send explicit messages to females in the online community. Members of the Eye try to maintain a high standard of ethics, if only to keep the higher ground.

But I was still waiting for the Baroness's response. She wrote to me quickly after I sent her my first couple of messages, but then I had to wait for days to hear back from her. I wrote back with questions but I didn't receive a response. Maybe she wasn't open to speaking with a journalist, or maybe she just didn't have the time — although, I doubted it since she was always on Facebook.

The Golden Don had a freaky mask: gold and sculpted with details that gave him a serious and dangerous look. With his long dark cape, he gave me the impression of being a real criminal. In a picture in the company of other "teammates," he was the most imposing, partly because of his height.

I wrote to the Golden Don, and he quickly replied:

> Being a Real Life Super Villain means something differ-ent to each individual. Expectations are applied and can scarcely be lived up to. I do not plan crimes or wish pain or suffering on anyone.
>
> In the comic book world, superheroes are a response and, in a way, rise up to fight supervillains. In the Real Life Super Hero community, Real Life Super Villains are a direct response to the sometimes preposterous and egomaniacal efforts and actions of those who call them-selves "superheroes."
>
> I am a member of a villain group — the Roaming Eye of Doom. We are a tightly knit band of like-minded people bent on world domination. We use a good amount of humor in our message to reach the commu-nity at large. We will not hesitate to challenge someone who we feel is making false claims or is acting in a way that is less than "heroic." We feel when you say you are a "hero" you had damned better act that way. We make

videos to be funny and mock heroes to spread what we want to say. We also walk a fine line so as not to alienate our audience. Because deep down we are all hungry for attention, but we don't let that get in the way of our ruthless nature.

Along with several other factors, since the Roaming Eye of Doom has been in full operation, the behavior in the Facebook Community for the Real Life Super Heroes has changed dramatically. False stories are fewer and accounts of inappropriate behavior have dropped dramatically.

If a message to young people from villains were to be given from us, it would be to *not* participate in Real Life Super Hero activity. Most of these people are playing dress-up and would do much more for their community by simply organizing neighborhood watch or volunteering their time to charity. Some "heroes" acknowledge they are partially in it for the fun, and I respect their straightforwardness. Usually these people are sincere and draw no ire from us at the Roaming Eye of Doom.

All hail the Eye!
Thank you for your interest,
The Golden Don.

I found his communication genuine and well-written. I was impressed by his clarity, and by his writing, which was very down-to-earth for a guy in a golden mask, and by something else ...

I thanked him, told him I was going to patrol with some superheroes, and asked him who I should avoid.

"There are some I have heard rumours about, but I would be remiss to speak on hearsay.... However, if there are a few names of some you are planning to meet, I can give you my opinion of them."

We discussed a few superheroes I was thinking of meeting, and he would not give me information on them unless his facts were verified. He gave me the names of a few I should avoid — not surprisingly, the same names that always came up each time I asked that question. Then I asked him about Death's Head Moth, the superhero who was supposed to accompany me during my stay with the Virginia Initiative.

"I wish I had details about him. He is not very active in the hero community online as I have seen. I can research him and get more information for you gladly."

A question was boiling inside of me. I hadn't asked anyone else, so I felt very uncomfortable asking for his age. But again, the way he communicated, compared to others, made me very curious.

"I am 35," he wrote. "Too old for this nonsense, but I have always needed a creative outlet and have never found one. I am very artistic (I made my mask) and have always enjoyed utilizing my way with people and my darker side … this is like my art."

We were the same age. I was surprised to find that villains ranged from about 18 years old up to their 40s. I could tell from their writing that age made a difference in their responses.

The Golden Don wrote back to me later that same day. "Hello. Death's Head Moth comes up okay. However, I would suggest that going on patrol with these people might create complications, no matter how noble their intentions are."

I was fully aware of that since many heroes had warned me. Of course, when patrolling with crime fighters, I was taking chances.

I thanked him again, before laughing at his last comment: "Glad to be of service.… But remember: I am not nice. I am a horrible villain. Ha!"

⚡

In addition to heroes and villains, the online community has a fair number of out-and-out trolls. These are people who, hiding behind the anonymity of the Internet, will lash out, presumably because they are starved for attention. One of these trolls found out what I was working on, and he decided to reach out to me. I found out first-hand what it was like to be bullied, harassed, and threatened by an individual who wanted to make my life a living hell.

"You barely took notice and for that you'll pay. Soon it will be time to pay the piper. I'll get you, my pretty. And your little dog, too," the troll wrote.

My encounter with the troll was a little scary, but nobody else in the community seemed to take him too seriously as a threat. He was just some lonely, attention-starved loser. The sad part is that if he had approached me under his real RLSH or RLSV profile, I would have given him the attention he wanted.

Nonetheless, it was nice to see that both villains and heroes responded to this threat. When I posted it on my Facebook wall, they all reacted. Supervillains and superheroes apologized to me, telling me I should not have to face those "failures." Hazmat, a RLSH who had shared his point of view with me regarding weapons, even made a YouTube video where he apologized to me for the actions of these troubled people.

That said, it showed that both heroes and villains can attract jealousy and envy. After all, trolls are only bullies. As explained by a licensed therapist on GoodTherapy.org, bullies are "usually people with low self-esteem and a certain amount of unconscious resentment (envy, jealously) that pushes the bully to project their own feelings of inadequacy onto you while denying that anything is wrong with them."[*]

But I didn't know that somewhere, a stranger was looking out for me.

---

[*] Roni Weisberg-Ross, "The Basics of Bullying and How to Stop It," *GoodTherapy. org*, www.goodtherapy.org/blog/adult-bullies.

5

THANATOS

I was on my way to meet with the personification of death: Thanatos, the Dark Avenger. Thanatos is one of the oldest — if not the oldest — superheroes, and one of the most respected men in the community. He's also from my own country.

Dressed like a cross between a cowboy and an undertaker, Thanatos patrols the streets of Vancouver, British Columbia, where the prostitutes, drug dealers, and homeless people of Vancouver congregate. For almost 10 years, now in his 60s, he has been speaking to people, helping them, and getting them water, blankets, and food in an effort to help alleviate their hardship. Before becoming a superhero, Thanatos patrolled the streets as a civilian. But just like his contemporary, Life from New York, people would not remember him. Today, nobody forgets his appearance. His grim face of death speaks to the importance of life.

I remembered my first job as a journalist at a website company. It gave me the opportunity to interview NHL players about their personal lives. The company was located on Hastings Street, the same street Thanatos patrols. I remembered how dirty the street was and how unsafe I felt when I was going to work and coming back home, even during daylight hours. I couldn't even imagine how it was at night. But years later, the night before I met with Thanatos, I decided to see Hastings Street at night — the way he sees it.

It was just after dark, around 9 p.m., and I was wearing my bullet-proof vest, carrying the tactical flashlight given to me by Death's Head Moth, and, of course, my cellphone. I didn't bring a camera, as Thanatos had told me how dangerous that could be. When he is being filmed for a documentary, he makes his patrols during the daytime, in safer places where cameras are more tolerated. Although it might seem foolish, I also wore a fake wedding ring. Because of my work on serial killers, I was well aware that predators usually prefer to attack people who have no attachments and no one, such as a husband, to report them missing. But why take a chance? I wore my contacts instead of my glasses, in case there was a scuffle. I wore small earrings, instead of ones that are easy to grab. My ID was in a pocket of my jeans that closed with a button. No purse, so nothing to steal or to grab on to. The Golden Don also knew when and where I was and was expecting to hear back from me when I got back to my room.

It was quite dark out by the time I reached Hastings Street. I saw a huge, tall man who was probably twice my size. From his worn clothes, dirty, long hair, and long and unwashed beard that didn't seem to have been shaved in years, I suspected he was a transient. I looked at him, smiled, and said, "Excuse me?"

"WHAT?" he responded, with squinting eyes that matched his angry voice. I told him I was looking for a man named Thanatos. I described him and told him he helped people in need. The man's expression changed quickly, and he told me he didn't know him. I thanked him and moved on.

I walked on for a couple of blocks to where there were what seemed to be hundreds of people. I skirted around two fist fights, including one where the fighters seemed completely oblivious to the blows they were inflicting and receiving. I was being very cautious, and I watched the crowd as much as they were watching me.

"Excuse me," I said to a tall, long-haired, tough-looking guy standing on his own. "Do you know who Thanatos is?"

"Who?" he asked, with a leery gaze.

"The man dressed as death, who helps people," I answered.

"Ahhh! Yes," he said.

But even after I explained who I was and what I was doing, the man would only nod in response to my inquiries. This was going to be a long night.

Nearby, some people appeared to be buying drugs, others were selling, and some appeared to be selling stolen goods. I asked some locals if they knew anything about Thanatos. Although some of them didn't know his name, many people knew who I meant, but no one wanted to talk about him. It was like they were protecting Thanatos.

A smiling, suspicious-looking man who had just collected money approached me and asked me who I was looking for. I told him, and he asked around, but no one had any information for me. He gave me a slightly eerie grin and told me to come back to him if I needed anything else.

Finally I found someone who was willing to talk about Thanatos. She was one of the few women on the street, and she was selling goods. I asked her if she knew the superhero. "Yes," she said nervously. She was an aboriginal woman with black hair. Her skin was so deeply wrinkled and lined that she looked like she was in her 70s. She was perhaps only about 45, but the signs of a harsh and difficult life were all over her. She smoked her cigarette and told me that she had to concentrate on watching out for the police. She was selling sunglasses and assorted bric-a-brac on the corner. One pair of glasses was even missing a lens. She was nervous about being distracted by me and suggested we meet the following day, but she wouldn't tell me her name. I didn't think she'd show up to any future appointment, and I had no way to track her down again. I practically begged her for two minutes of her time and promised to be discreet and inconspicuous. She finally agreed.

The woman's head darted around as she spoke, keeping a wary watch over her surroundings. She told me about the first time she saw Thanatos. "Well, his appearance freaked me out, but he is a very, very, solid man." When I asked if she ever spoke to him, she answered, "Well, yeah. I am here every day, for like … too long." She wasn't specific about what they talked about, but confirmed that he spoke with a lot of people and that he was very friendly. I thanked her when I saw she had nothing else to say.

Word had apparently spread that I was asking around for Thanatos. As I was leaving the woman, two tall and imposing men, dressed in dark black and blue, approached me. I found them initially intimidating, but they were actually just eager to heap praise on Thanatos, calling him "an amazing man."

The next day, I received an email from Thanatos: "Mountain View Cemetery, entrance off of 33rd Street. Just west of Fraser. Google it and use the TransLink website for bus directions. Meet at one thirty. I'll have the phone on as well, so you can call me."

A cab dropped me off at the cemetery, and I waited for the man who looks like death. A light rain was falling, turning the sky grey. I wasn't sure if it was the cold, damp, December air or the eerily isolated cemetery making me shiver. After about 20 minutes of waiting, I saw a person walking toward me. The tall figure wearing a black hat, a long black coat, and a black tie adorned with skulls could only be one person. And although I was alone with death in a cemetery, I couldn't have felt any safer.

We were talking and going deeper into the cemetery while I was trying to set up a video camera. Thanatos was doing the same thing; as he was making sure his camera worked, he asked me to say my name. Although I answered, I never imagined he would put that video on YouTube, or I would have been a little more original.

Continuing our walk through the headstones, we started the interview.

Thanatos began: "I help the homeless on the street with handouts of simple things like a loaf of bread, sometimes something as simple as a human touch and companionship. I watch what's going on with them and I draw attention to the plague of people who fall through the system and end up on the streets. In my city alone, I've probably reached out and touched six hundred people. Most of the people I look for are the people that aren't on the mainstream grid of receiving aid and help from the kitchens or the missions. Maybe they don't match the criteria to get in, there are barriers to them, they've squirrelled themselves away. So I go out and find them, where they've hidden away, and give them what they need and give them that companionship."

"But why the costume?" I asked.

"At first, it was very difficult. I couldn't get anyone's attention. Nobody wanted to listen. One day, a police officer told me, 'You know, people on the street really have nothing better to look forward to other than death.'

That really stunned me. So, I said, 'If that is the case, then death is going to have to get out there and start taking care of these people.' I was brought up on comic books. I'm a horror buff as well. So I modernized the figure and took elements from the Shadow and the Green Hornet and put them together. I had the same thought they had in *Kick-Ass*: 'Why can't someone be a superhero and do this?' I started doing research and I found there are all kinds of people doing this."

Today he wasn't wearing his utility belt, simply because we were going to patrol together, and he didn't want to have any trouble.

He continued: "I think Super Hero down in Florida said it the best: 'We fight apathy.' We get people motivated, we inspire them, and we show them that one person can make a difference."

As we were discussing what he does, I could not help but feel sorry for the homeless, especially for those who are rejected by their own families. The superhero was recalling a time when one homeless man was being harassed by three well-off women. The women quickly left with their husbands in a cab when the RLSH approached them.

"His name was Samuel," Thanatos explained about the homeless man. "He lived down the street for over three years. When I went to reach out my hand to shake his hand and introduce myself, he pulled back and said, 'I'm full blown!' Full-blown means that he has full-blown AIDS. I told him that was okay. He's in the dying stage, which can take three to five years. I said, 'I'm not worried. You can't catch full-blown AIDS from contact by hand.' So I gave him my hand to shake, and he held it very tightly. He was almost crying. He told me that nobody had touched him in three years. All he needed was some human contact. So I talked to him for a little bit, and I got him a coffee and some sandwiches. That kept him going. He thanked me and said that I really made him feel like a person again. So there's an example of something simple that anyone can do."

I liked Thanatos's sense of humour, too. Using his dramatic persona as a tool, he was told that three different people had quit drugs after meeting him because he scared the hell out of them when he woke them up to give them food. "One fellow got tired of death coming to help him survive and figured he better get off or death was going to come for him pretty soon."

"He asked me why I was dressed up," said Thanatos, talking about another homeless man, "and I said 'I represent death because death walks the streets of Vancouver and takes homeless people.' Every day on Hasting Street, three to four people die of anything from violence, overdoses, poisons, thirst, to hunger. The cemetery is full of them."

"What do you tell them to help them?" I asked.

"There was a fella who was living under a bridge, in a space of about seven or eight cubic feet. A small refrigerator box is the space he had. He was in his late 50s. When I found him four years ago, he'd been living there already for four years. He rarely came out. He was under-nourished, dehydrated a lot of the time, and very reclusive. It took a year to get him to tell me his name. It took me two more years to get him to come out and start sleeping outside. He asked me why I dress up like this and do it. 'Don't people just laugh at you?' he asked. I said, 'Yeah, until I tell them why.' I said, 'The police believe that you guys have nothing better to live for than death.' I told him that on a Wednesday, and Thursday morning he went to a social worker and said he was from the province of Saskatchewan and would like a bus ticket to go back home to his family. He told the social worker about me and he said that things I had told him and done made sense. He said he was scared of dying alone."

Thanatos cares. "The Bible tells us that we are supposed to take care of our brothers. What you do for my brothers, you do to me as well. We should be looking out for each other. I've seen these people, I've talked to them, I've heard their stories, and they don't want to be there. Most of them didn't intend to be on the street.

"Social workers say that they see these people in the morning and people don't remember them by the afternoon. They forget the social worker's name and what they look like. But they remember the crazy guy with a mask out there helping. I tried talking to people. I tried talking to the press about things down here. Nobody came to see me. I put on a mask, and I have people all interested. I've had people from France, Germany, from all over the States come to talk to me because I put on a mask and I'm drawing attention to the problem. There's people out there that say this is an ego trip. If this was an ego trip, would I hide behind the mask?"

It made sense to me. Some RLSHs do have inflated egos. The motivation can go from helping others to becoming popular. And often those people who take off their masks just want to be known and seen. Thanatos is obviously different, and it is one of the reasons he is so respected.

"What's it like becoming Thanatos?" I asked.

"It's a development that superheroes all go through. We're going to take on this superhero identity. We see our real identity and our new identity as two separate entities. After a while, we find out that even when we are not costumed up, we are stepping in. If we see something, we call it in. We take action. For a while, it feels like our superhero personality is taking over our lives. Then as we go along, we realize that we were always like that."

Thanatos noticed the homeless when he worked on Hastings Street as a groundskeeper, taking care of a couple of buildings. He explained that after being on the street for a while, many people turn to drugs to escape the harsh reality. They get caught up in it, with no one to point them in the right direction. "It's like some of them need to be taken by the hand and integrated back into society. And until we are ready to do that and stop them from ending up there, there's going to be the problems." He followed with a great example of a conversation he'd had with a homeless man.

"I've had one fella actually stop dealing drugs because I talked to him one day and I asked him why he was doing this. He said, 'For the money, man.' I said, 'Really. So you got a big condo, pool, and everything?' He said, 'No.' I said, 'Well, you got a great car, a Maserati, or a Ferrari?' He said, 'No. I don't have a car.' I said, 'A bike?' He went, 'No.' I said, 'How about a mountain bike?' He said, 'No, not even that.' So I said, 'I thought you were in it for the money.' He stood there and he said, 'Yeah, so did I.' A few days later, people told me that he had just quit. Sometimes, it's just about saying the right thing at the right time."

Thanatos couldn't have a better caring example than his own parents. Their patience and dedication is exemplified by their own story. On December 7, 1941, when they were just dating, they heard about the attack on Pearl Harbor. The next day, Thanatos's father enlisted in the army. The couple drove to Reno that night and got married. They had only one week together until they saw each other again five years later, and they have stayed together ever since.

Following family tradition, Thanatos served in the military for six years. He was an intelligence officer in the United States Special Forces. He went to Vietnam, simply because he cared. "I thought we were doing something when I first went over. I thought we were doing something right. And trying to help," he said. But "the harsh reality of what was going on caused me to have to just disagree with the U.S. government and their political position."

Back home, the superhero continued his patrols a different way ... on the street. And although it might not compare to the jungles of Vietnam, patrolling is a very risky undertaking. About 18 years ago in Toronto, Thanatos saw a gang robbing a store. The men were armed with knives and hand-guns. The superhero went in with a machete, not to hurt them, but to get them mad and to get them to chase him outside the store so that the owners inside — a couple — would live. Although the thieves stayed inside, Thanatos kept them sequestered until the police arrived, arrested them, and charged them. They also found out that the criminals were wanted in other provinces, one of them for murder in Quebec.

Thanatos wasn't afraid for his life. He explained, "I've been shot before in combat. I've had shootouts in combat in the army. And as a police officer in Rhodesia. And in Zimbabwe. I was a constable there with the British South Africa Police. A handgun has a very short axis of radius. So if you move it even a little bit, by the time the bullet gets to the target that slight movement is multiplied out to several feet. So they end up shooting wide. But I'm not always the brightest Real Life Super Hero out there. Down at a park, there was a fellow who was yelling at me, on the other side of the street, 'Get your ass out of my turf. I don't want you here!' And I said, 'Tough!' He reached into his pocket and pulled out a clip, so I realized he had a gun, and he took out a bullet and he threw it at me. He said, 'Next time, I'm going to put that in the right way.' I was staring at him and I said, 'Go ahead! I'm here now. What's stopping you? Take your best shot, but make it good.' And he just came to retrieve it."

Thanatos, like almost all superheroes, wears a bulletproof and stab-proof vest. It's a 3A, just like the one I purchased in Virginia.

But even if this superhero faces threats, his family supports him in his desire to patrol. Today he lives with his wife and 17-year-old daughter, who is very mature for her age. Just like her father, she volunteers on her own.

And Thanatos's wife often patrols with him, staying far behind, making sure that the RLSH is okay.

While we were on the subject of family, I asked him to tell me more about his siblings and his childhood. With his father being in military intelligence, many of his childhood experiences made him a strong boy, including living all over the southern states of Mississippi, Kentucky, West Virginia, Virginia, Georgia, and Texas. He moved every 12 to 14 months during his first 12 years. Although it wasn't hard for him to make new friends, he reports, "I got to see a lot of racism. And we're an Irish family and we saw a lot of racism towards us. So I understood what that was and how wrong it was." It shaped his thinking in many ways. He doesn't judge. At one point, his mother decided it would be better for the children to live in one place and go to one high school, so they moved to their grand-parent's house in Santa Monica, California. Aside from that, his parents were great, but he did have a sister he didn't get along with. "My sister and I fought like dogs and cats, literally. We both have scars to prove it." She is a year older than he is, and they never seemed to get along. Since she moved to Brazil, they are "happy," he said. They still love each other in their own way.

As we walked around the cemetery under the grey sky, the superhero decided he would bring me to where he patrols. We left the dead and re-entered the world of the living — even if some of them were barely holding on. "I will show you the Downtown Eastside. It's not always what you see, or what you think you're seeing. It can be very deceptive, a very dangerous place. We're going to go undercover, so you won't be filming during that. But I'll show you a lot of stuff there, so it will be very interesting."

Since his answers were very important to me, I asked him if we could record him by putting the mini-recorder I had brought in his pocket. He didn't mind, so we tested it, and it worked.

As we approached the bus stop across the street, the disguised Thanatos surprised me by taking off his mask, providing a glimpse of some of his 112 tattoos. He has always collected tattoos, and his tattoos were hard to miss. He was also a tattoo artist and still practises on the side. But the most distracting things were the dark circles around his eyes. He usually puts black makeup around his eyes, although he didn't do that today. I could see that the fabric of his mask had absorbed some of the black makeup he usually wears and it had smeared on his face.

He looks like a stereotypical criminal, but Thanatos says he has never been to prison. He has, however, been arrested a few times when trying to defend people — like when he stopped the store robbery. "They dismissed the charges and the Crown attorney just blew up at the cops for charging me." But he was charged with possession of prohibited weapons because he had nunchaku, and he didn't know that they were illegal in Canada. He had to pay a fine and had a probation period.

The story I found the most reprehensible was that he had a price on his head in South Vietnam. "The Viet Cong had a price on me. I ran a network that reached all the way up into North Vietnam of informants, for the government. And we were able to organize a pretty good effect of strikes against them and the whole Ho Chi Minh trail. Their intelligence was as good as ours, so they knew who I was."

However, Thanatos was not afraid. He was honoured. "Not everybody gets a price put on their head. Like the guy in *Star Wars*, I had a death sentence in six systems and a price on my head for a while." But today he feels safe. That 1967 regime doesn't exist anymore.

The bus arrived. When we boarded, the bus was nearly empty, and we sat in the back. This gave us the opportunity to continue our discussion with more privacy. I felt lucky to meet with this masked crusader. In the RLSH community, he is perceived as the best example, the role model, the patriarch, in the community.

> Nadia Fezzani (NF): Every time I interview someone in the RLSH community, they ask me if I have interviewed you and tell me that I should.
> Thanatos (Than): I keep a level head. I don't argue with people. I don't fight. I try to do what I consider good for the entire community. Talking about the community, Phoenix is really looking forward to taking you out on patrol. He's a media favourite right now. Some people love him; some people hate him. I'm telling people that they are not thinking. Years ago, we had a debate going on about the media, and I told people that at some point,

the media was going to pick one of us, is just going to
be all over that person, and it's not going to be who they
want. That's what happened. They say, "Oh, he's a media
whore and he's getting all of the attention and getting
all of the press." But every time he does something, my
inbox fills up. I've had schools contact me because they
were watching the news and googled it, as they wanted
to know if there were any in Canada. They found me.
Everybody is that way. As soon as Phoenix does something, everybody in the community starts to get requests.
When he starts getting interviews, things start coming
down. It's good, whether others like him or not. Yes, he
draws attention to himself, but he draws attention to all
of us in the long run.

On several occasions, I witnessed jealousy in the community. The way
some RLSHs become aggressive and offensive with other RLSH was sometimes hard to believe: deleting Facebook friends because they are friends
with another superhero they don't like, insults, threats. I heard that one
superhero had called many employers of superheroes and gotten them
fired, simply because he didn't agree with them giving their real names
to other superheroes. I had heard many other things, but that report had
been repeated to me over and over again.

NF: Thanatos, do you think there is jealousy in the community?
Than: In some cases, yes. Some people think that getting media attention is the big thing and that it's a lot
of fun. No offence, but it sucks. I get so tired of telling
the same story over and over again. It starts to get to
you after a while; it also starts to get in the way of some
of the things you are trying to do. But RLSHs want to
be in the media, they want to see their persona in the
paper for some reason, and their nose gets out of joint
when it isn't. They get very upset with Peter Tangen
if he hasn't photographed them. It upsets them. Peter

picked who he wanted to do for the imagery. He wants a specific type of imagery to present to the public, so some people didn't get picked. It doesn't mean that he likes them any less, it just means that he wanted certain imagery, and he explained it. It's an interesting community because there are so many egos and so many people who believe wholeheartedly in what they are doing. And they are willing to die for what they believe in, and they don't realize that other people have a different way of doing things. They get very self-centred, and so they start putting down something different that is being done by someone else. They've got to understand that we are all working together. I like to call it the ripple effect, if everyone is taking care of their little corner of the world, they will connect and things will get a little bit better.

But it's going to happen. It's human nature. This is the real world and people have real personalities, real crashes, and personal problems with other people. When Martin Luther King was starting the black movement and getting it going, not everyone got along like angels. They split into two groups. Malcolm X had one group and Martin Luther King had the other. I'm sure Benjamin Franklin and George Washington did not see eye to eye all the time. It happens. I would like to see them stop it, though. It is counterproductive. At some point, a lot of people realized this. A lot of these people I've met are very smart at what they do, and they are realizing that arguing, burning bridges, is not getting anywhere. You've got to work together as a team and take what comes.

NF: That's what happened with Phoenix and another member of the community. That member was really upset because of the pepper-spray story.

Than: They have a lot in common and they have a common ground.

That member had criticized Jones on Facebook. Then he said they were talking. Then it was another attack. And then it was another Real Life Super Hero, Motor Mouth, who was heavily condemned by the same member.

As we talked about Motor Mouth, we got to the topic of the event with his teammate, the Ray. A 22-year-old from Oakland, the Ray was in Motor Mouth's team. He had attacked a police officer who tried to hit a couple who was kissing. The Ray used a shield to defend the civilians and himself. He was arrested and allegedly beaten by police officers and knocked unconscious. Many RLSHs felt that Motor Mouth was responsible for what happened since the Ray was new to the superhero world and left unsupervised.

> Than: Motor Mouth is quite the character. He lives up to his name. That man does not stop talking. That's his superpower. If there is a superpower, he's got it, and it's the ability to just keep on talking, but he's actually saying something. He is very deep and that man has got a heart that just will not stop. He cares for people. And he's a great guy, he's a lot of fun and takes what he is doing very seriously and tries to do the best.
>
> The Ray was doing what he thought was good. He had the right to be there. But it was just a bad situation; Occupied movements get way out of hand so easily and he got caught in the middle of it.
>
> NF: Did you know that the two of them build armour?
>
> Than: A lot of people are into armour and making different things.
>
> NF: Certain guys get upset about that.
>
> Than: Yes, some people believe that you shouldn't carry any form of self-defence weapon at all, and if you have to carry something, then you are doing it wrong. Yes, the weapons become toys and everyone has got to buy all of the toys they can, but they are trying to use them effectively and properly. It's a tough line.
>
> NF: What do you personally think?

Than: People say you don't need the weapons or the protection, but you do. It's dangerous out here. I have had
guns flashed at me, knives, every kind of sharp instrument
you can imagine.

Indeed, patrolling can be very dangerous, as I learned when I found
out that Phoenix Jones had been stabbed before. As we talked about the
community, Thanatos brought up HOPE, the yearly event in San Diego
where many superheroes meet and distribute goods to homeless people.
That event gave him the opportunity to work with several partners, such as
DC's Guardian, Dark Guardian, and Geist. Thanatos also meets often with
Phoenix Jones. They do not live far from each other, and they are often
the two people who are requested for TV interviews on the West Coast.

Next we talked about the villains. "I talk to all of them," he said. "The
villains came about to critique our community and expose the people
who were frauds. They exposed people who would be a liability to the
whole movement."

Also, some superheroes start young. I was contacted by some of them
who were 15, 16, 17 years old. The last one was from Vancouver. He wanted to meet with Thanatos and me, but I didn't feel comfortable bringing a
minor with me on patrol.

Thanatos knew exactly who I was talking about. "He lives in a halfway
house environment or foster home. He seems like his heart is in the right
place, but he hasn't really trained or done anything. It's too young to be
doing certain things."

Another one in Canada is 17 years old. He doesn't fight crime directly. He organizes handouts, and he has spoken at a couple of schools and
colleges about the RLSHs. He fights crime by calling emergency services.
People tell him to keep doing what he's doing.

"The police say the biggest complaint is that we are undertrained,"
Thanatos said. "In the HBO documentary, the officer went on about how
we are unprepared and untrained. But in most cases, in the United States
especially, there are a lot of us with military backgrounds, Green Berets,
Navy Seals, former police officers, active police officers, people that have
had training, people who are martial arts experts. This movement attracts
everyone. We're not crazy people. We've had a sociologist explain that on TV."

Indeed, they did. In the HBO documentary *Superheroes*, Robin Rosenberg, a clinical psychologist and expert on the psychology of superheroes, both real-life and fictional, said this:

> Real Life Super Heroes aren't necessarily crazier than you or I or anyone else. They take the instance of superheroes for real; what would it be like. They are dedicated to what they do. It's a hobby, for most people, because it's not a paying job, and it's a hobby they've thrown themselves into passionately, and they are also doing good at the same time.
>
> We all have alter egos. We don't all dress in costumes.
>
> For Real Life Super Heroes, they may have experienced significant adversity or trauma that left them with a sense of mission and purpose. Often the answer that they end up finding is: this happened to me for a reason and it is so that I can do good.
>
> There's some psychological research on masking and people report feeling more anonymous in the sense that they feel less like their usual selves, so it's easier in the sense that by donning the costume they are allowing their alter ego — if you will — to come out more readily. To take a traumatic event and find meaning from it by wanting to do good for others is a wonderful gift both to oneself and to other people.

We arrived at our destination, and got off the bus on Hastings Street. Thanatos explained, "This is the oldest Chinatown in North America — not the largest, but it is the oldest. We are going to walk through. Vancouver has quite the history."

As we got off the bus, we heard someone talking in the background. It was a man selling his artwork on the street. From his attire, it was easy to tell he didn't sell these pieces just for fun. Thanatos stopped to talk with him.

> Than: Nice drawings. I have no place to keep it my friend. [Thanatos handed him some loose change.] Just because you are a good artist, man.

Artist: Oh! Thank you so much!
Than: Take care. What's your name?
Artist: They call me Dan. I draw here all the time. Look
me up one day and I will draw what you want.
Than: Okay, I will.

Moving on, Thanatos told me more about the man: "He's a fixture around here. He makes what he can. Gets drunk all the time. Drugs, not a really big deal. A lot of people use drugs because they have to get away from the realities."

We arrived at the building I had passed the previous night, across the street from the people I had spoken to, and the unmasked crusader explained to me where we were. "This is the main pot area for the city. If you want it, you come down here. The Carnegie Centre is there, on the corner."

That was the building. A former library that had been built in the early 1900s. It's now the community centre. "People are just hanging around there," Thanatos said.

It had such beautiful, old architecture. I wished we still built like that instead of the modern, cold, straight-windowed edifices of today. I hadn't taken the time to observe it last night when I was alone in what people call a bad area.

Walking down to the area favoured by dealers of harder drugs, I told Thanatos about the night I came here.

NF: On my way down here, I stopped one guy and started asking questions about you and he wouldn't answer.
It's like he thought I was a cop trying to get information
about you.
Than: They are loyal.
NF: I was surprised though, as I thought everybody would
know who you are.
Than: A lot of people, from what I've heard from the
police, have heard about me from a lot of people.

I had no doubt about it. Thanatos has been in the media enough to be known in his area.

"This is really the edge of the area," Thanatos said. "The black guy standing there is a heroin dealer. I have seen him arrested a score of times. I've seen guns, knives, and one day a short spear taken off him. This is Canada's poorest postal code. At some point, I think the decision was made to just let it go. And it just got out of hand. The petty crime rate out here is through the roof. People will steal anything. There are just too many people out here to do anything about it. It would just flood the court system and the courts would just throw them back out onto the street. See this guy, here? In that bag, he's either got drugs or money. Most of these guys, who are just standing around doing nothing, are dealers."

Thanatos explained that since there could be six hundred people here — which was not hard to believe after the enormous crowd I had seen the previous night — it would be too hard for him to give things away. So he goes to other locations, some where people are hiding, other locations where people with no roof are hanging out.

Just then, I saw the woman I had spoken to on my previous visit. I told Thanatos about it. She was still selling stuff. Same nervous body language. Same watchful look in her eyes.

"Something is going down between the guy with the hoodie and the guy with the coat right now. They're hiding things. They deal everything along there," said Thanatos.

"I spoke to those guys over there," I said, showing who I meant with my eyes only.

"This is a very dangerous area. They've had people knifed here; it happens quite often. They've had shootouts."

I told Thanatos about the crazy fights I had seen when I was here last. They didn't seem like fights that would be easily separated. It looked like there had to be a winner, no matter the cost. I didn't know if someone would pull a knife. I definitely didn't want to walk close by. He told me about a riot that happened a long time ago here. Without any cops around, he had yelled, "Cops! Cops!" waving his hands running down the street. "That's effective," he said.

Thanatos explained that the area we were in supported about three thousand people living on the streets, using the shelters and the system, and just living on the street because "they just can't get into the places. Everything is barred heavily, security is a prime consideration. Lots of small petty crime taking place, so everyone tries to protect their property." The drug dealers utilize a system similar to what I'd seen elsewhere. The pusher would call someone on his cell and that person would give the dope to the customer.

Their security, according to Thanatos, is provided by aboriginals. "They're not drinking. They're not selling. They're watching. They'll sit there sometimes with what looks like a bottle of wine, and it's really water or lemonade. At least one of them will have a gun right now. And they're watching out for the people on this side of the street. This is hell's alley. If hell had an address, this would be it."

It took the superhero four years to be able to walk down the alley without seeming like a threat. It took him time and patience. In hot weather, he would give bottles of water. Food and gloves during the winter. He kept telling people he didn't judge them.

At this moment, a police car went by. "That's a homicide," said Thanatos. "Supervisors don't go with their lights on, unless it's a homicide. Going up Fraser, in that direction, it is probably gang-related."

"See the guy with blue gloves?" he said. "It's because he is selling methamphetamine raw, but he doesn't have a pack. He's wearing the gloves so he doesn't contaminate himself with the drug."

Though there is a police station close by, the criminals aren't afraid of it.

"People will shoot up there, smoke crack, perform sex," said Thanatos. "Some of these people have lived on the streets for years. People die here because of knives and drug overdose. One guy wrapped himself up in plastic wrap, fell asleep, and suffocated. Down the street, a 17-year-old man overdosed on drugs and drowned in a puddle of water about half an inch deep. In the sub-basement of the parking garage here, a fellow starved to death. He got too weak to get out of there and died. These streets have the rule of threes, and they are very simple: three minutes without air, three days without water, three weeks without food, and you die. And people die like that all the time. Some of these people have mental problems, some of them have mental problems brought on by drug abuse. Some are just trying to escape.

"This is a place I go into at different times when I'm undercover. You can buy just about anything in there: pills, guns, women, small children. Slavery exists in Canada, it exists in North America, and people just don't realize it. Pimps get a hold of girls at no matter what age, they get them hooked on drugs. Now they have leverage, they own that woman, they own that person, they make that person go out, work, and have sex, give them the money. In return they get just enough drugs to keep them hooked, to keep them obedient."

Thanatos can spend entire days here, sometimes every day of the week, 15 to 20 hours a week. He still tries his best to balance family life, work, and the patrol.

"When I'm with my family, I am with my family watching movies, playing games, etc. We are very old-fashioned and a tight group. When I started, my wife told me, 'Make sure you don't forget us.' So I always try not to. She understands that I want the world better for my daughter, I want the world better for my wife, I want the world better for my descendants, if any."

Home is also his refuge. When he is overwhelmed and needs a break, he takes a few days to spend time with his family, do fun things, and relax. "The urge always comes back," he said.

When it's time for patrols, he sometimes prowls in costume, sometimes not. When he doesn't wear his gear, he observes and reports any trends he sees. "I've been able to tip the police so that they have an idea of what's out there on the street."

I was surprised that he was willing to make that information public. I asked him if that could potentially harm him.

"It's sort of understood, as far as the people on the street are concerned," he said. He reports what's happening. "If someone needs an ambulance, I'll call an ambulance. If someone is assaulted, I'll call the police for them. I was an intelligence officer, so I know how to observe and put things together."

But duties also take him all over the place at times. "I've been borrowed by a company to [go to] New Orleans after Katrina to help pick up all the dead people," he said. "It was completely unreal. I'd never seen anything like that in my life. It was overwhelming, but we did some good. We had people and families thanking us. My first day there, the National Guard asked me where I was from. I said, 'Vancouver.' He said, 'You all came down from Canada, all the way here to help us?' He cried, hugged me, and thanked me. It's rewarding when people say thanks. Little things start to mean a lot. Peter has been out with me and has seen people come up and hug me."

We kept walking and talking, with Thanatos pointing out people of interest in between recounting his memories. He told me about a woman named Maria and her husband. "They had five children. They left Guatemala after their oldest son stepped on a land mine and was killed. So they walked up here. They had four children with them when they left, two died on the route … the trip, hardship, weather, extremes. The other two smaller children were taken into family services and granted refugee status. Maria and her husband could not get welfare or get any aid, so they ended up on the street. They got into drugs. He ran off with another woman. She got into prostitution so she could have money to live on. She got into drugs to get away from the prostitution and get it out of her head. They found her in an alleyway, under a mattress, behind a dumpster where she had died probably a week earlier."

In the summer, there are a lot more people. One day, when the super-hero was giving away bottles of water to people, he approached a drug dealer who was sitting on a chair. As Thanatos reached out to give him the water, he noticed the man had a gun. "A very nice nickel-plated Walther PPK pistol. That is a James Bond gun, 380 calibre, they don't come nickel-plated very often," said Thanatos. As the dealer looked at the masked man like he wanted to kill him, Thanatos told him, "Be cool, man. I'm just giving you water." The dealer asked, "Why are you giving me water?" Thanatos answered that it was because it was hot. They talked together about the dealer's personal life and still do today.

We continued our interview.

> NF: How do you feel when you get threatened?
> Than: I feel the adrenalin. The threat is very real down here. I have to be prepared.
> NF: Do you like the challenge?
> Than: I could live without it quite well, without that threat, that fear, but it wouldn't get things done. Sometimes, you have to put yourself on the line. People ask, "Are you willing to die for your beliefs?" Yes, I am. I'd rather make my point than die for this belief, but I'm quite willing to put my life on the line.
> NF: How would you feel if you had to stop?

Than: I wouldn't. There's not a power on earth that could make me stop. I'm stubborn. I believe in what I'm doing and what others are doing in this as well. I just won't stop.

I know Thanatos responded to me, but I had to re-ask my question. That wasn't the answer I wanted to hear.

NF: I am going to ask you again. What if you *had* to stop tomorrow, if you didn't have the choice ... how would you feel?

Than: My mission is to cause a positive change in this area. I would feel like I'd let them down and failure to me is just not an option.

NF: Would you feel like there was a hole in your life?

Than: Oh, yes. It's become a part of my family's life that I do this and they have learned to care as I do. It's hard. You are seeing just how nasty and dangerous this area can be. But at the same time, as Super Hero says, it's a hell of a lot of fun. I've had some hilarious times down here. I've startled people and I've known it and played on it. I've gotten to do things and go to places.

Talking about nasty and dangerous, Thanatos's life could have been very different. In fact, the man under Thanatos's gear used to be a drinker. But one morning, 25 years ago, he showed up at work and witnessed an incident that changed his life. He did embalming for funeral homes when they were extra busy, and that day when he arrived in the prep room, he saw a couple in their mid-thirties who had both died in a car crash. "They had such a high level of alcohol in their blood that all you could smell was beer and liquor," he said. "In the next room were their six-year-old daughter and eight-year-old son. Both also killed in the car crash." Thanatos hasn't had a drink since.

Although the patrols are sometimes fun, it can be hard mentally. Thanatos spends his own money. Food, water, and most expenses come out of his pocket. He accepts donations, which helps, but $40 here and there can add up.

I asked him if he ever took a vacation. "I'd like to, but I don't," he replied. "My vacations come in little stages: going down to HOPE, in San Diego, going down to California like I did the other day for the interview. That's my little vacation. Hanging with Peter and Phoenix Jones. It doesn't get any better. We go to a restaurant. We go to a bar to meet some business people with Peter."

As Thanatos uttered these words, the woman I had interviewed the previous night left her spot.

"She's on her way to do something," said Thanatos. "Could be dinner, but ... nope ... she's meeting up. There's a deal. She's sold enough of her stuff to go buy a pipe. This is a place that operates just within the law. Most of the stuff they have in there is stolen. It's a well-known fence for stuff."

We were walking away from that street. It was time for us to go for a coffee, somewhere where, as Thanatos said, "It's a little bit safer."

On our way there, taking a break from the Hastings Street conversation, I took the opportunity to ask him about something I'd had on my mind for a while.

> NF: Thanatos, I am curious ... why did you want to meet in the cemetery?
>
> Than: One, because it fits my persona. It's a terrific backdrop. Two, I have a nice big open field to watch and see if anyone else is there. So it makes it perfectly safe for my identity to see me there. If I don't trust a person, they don't see me there. If I don't trust the person, then they don't see my face. You are one of very few.
>
> NF: Thank you, Thanatos! Have you ever had interview requests that you didn't trust?
>
> Than: I have always questioned their motives. We have had television shows in here wanting me on. They are the equivalent of Fox News, and I was not interested. Some journalists have been very unfair to us. They consider us comical geeks: we are stupid, we are fat kids living in our mother's basement, we are living a fantasy, we are

untrained, we don't know what we are doing. There are
a few superheroes who fit with that description. For the
most part, people know what they are doing. They know
their limits, they know their boundaries, they are trying
to do something good, and people do recognize them.
They had Razorhawk on Fox News and tried to make him
look stupid and it backfired. Razorhawk is someone who
is well-respected in the community.

Quite frankly, I wasn't surprised. After I wrote the article about
Phoenix Jones for the daily newspaper, some people called or wrote
to me, saying there was a TV show in Quebec that picked up the topic.
The guests they questioned were a psychologist and a police officer,
both living somewhere Real Life Super Heroes did *not* exist back then.
The "experts" seemed to categorize RLSHs as lunatics or delusional
people. My experience in the community was leading me to quite a
different conclusion.

⚡

After walking about 10 minutes, we got to a coffee shop in the more tour-
isty part of town. It was a small place, with a few tables. Thanatos gave me
a card, almost like a hockey card, that he had designed. He has several with
different pictures on it. He calls them his bundles.

He described their purpose: "On the back of it, I write 'friend,' so
they know that they've got somebody. At different times during my duties,
I had to go to the city morgue. I've had to sign out their bodies, see what
belongings they had. I've run into people that I have helped on the street
in the morgue, dead. And among their few belongings, they will have my
slips of paper. They hang on to them."

While the superhero is known in his area and all over the world, and
is often invited to appear on TV shows or to be interviewed on the radio,
for magazines, and for newspapers, there are many people who see the
human being and are not aware that he is Thanatos. "My neighbour still
has no idea of who I am and she's following [Thanatos] on Twitter and
on Facebook," he reports.

Thanatos wants to do more for the homeless, and being well-known can be of help. Now many people help him achieve his goals.

"I think you need a little bit of publicity to get the ball rolling. If people are willing to help me get the ball rolling, then I will keep it up. And then they got a story for the next year or so and they can just follow the progress on what we're doing, the progress of the street, how it's affecting the community and what kind of solutions we are coming up with."

But one person he tried to contact would not return his calls: the city mayor.

"I've sent him emails. I've phoned the office. I called him out on video — and that got mentioned in the newspapers with everything that I did — and he just does not respond. I've thought about just going up and waiting at city hall, and when he comes out, masking up and jumping out, saying, 'BOO!'"

We were talking about different ways a mayor could help make that part of the city better, from caring more about the Hastings area, to having people picking up needles, having more homeless shelters, and giving more assistance to those who need it. Security in Vancouver is an issue in many ways.

Than: Up by the 49th Street, there is a drug house going on, and they had a shootout one night and the bullets went through the wall. There was an Indo-Canadian family living next door. And the bullets almost grazed the grandmother. The grandmother had a heart attack, was taken to the hospital. She survived that, but she was never the same. We have a lot of gang problems and fighting in this city. One guy's girlfriend pulled out of her driveway and stopped at a sign on the street. Two guys walked up with machine guns and unloaded them into her head. Her two-year-old son, in the back, was injured when one of the bullets struck his Transformers toy — that got shattered and the plastic cut his cheek. They hit her because she was the girlfriend of a gang member. They got her boyfriend about a month later. In a crossfire, right in the middle of a mall parking lot, at 1 p.m., people were

walking their kids in and all of a sudden there was gun-
fire. This is a nasty world at times. There is just so much.
I know in my heart that one person can make a difference. If you look at history, it's always been one person
who's started something to make that difference. Gandhi,
Martin Luther King, Kennedy, Jesus, Muhammad, Buddha,
Einstein, Edison, Oppenheimer ... All of them are one
person and they made a difference.

NF: Are you religious?

Than: Yes. I consider myself a born-again Christian.
I just don't consider myself as someone who has to
shout "praise the Lord, Hallelujah!" every time somebody farts or does something stupid. I believe the best
way to teach the gospel of Jesus Christ isn't by talking,
but by doing, by setting an example that people can
recognize and say that is a Christian thing to do or
a very Muslim thing to do. One day, when we had a
very hot wave that was unbearable — at midnight, it
was still 109 degrees! — I found this couple who was
selling Arab scarves — also known as shemagh — by
the side of the road. There is no political or religious
significance to these. It's just a well-made scarf that
protects you from the weather.

[Thanatos showed me the black and white scarf he was
holding.]

Than: They were Middle Eastern. They came over here
to get a job, but they are refugees, so they cannot collect
unemployment. They were afraid to go to any Muslim
organization because in the Middle East it is very violent
and fascist, and one side doesn't talk to the other. I gave
the woman some water. She was almost dead. It took
four litres of water before she became coherent. So that
told me that she was pretty close. I put them in touch
with a Muslim group that I knew of that was very moderate. I posted on my blog about their story. This fella that
was following me and works for a very large concrete

company, tracked them down by phoning every Muslim group in the lower mainland and gave the husband a job paying $22 an hour.

The grateful couple then asked their saviour what they could do for him. He asked for one of their scarves. They agreed and asked again what else they could do for him. He answered, "Just do what you can. Remember where you were and help others." Now the woman volunteers through the mosque and does outreach in different parts of the city that have some of the same problems as in Thanatos's area.

> Than: Islam is very big on charity, and it is stressed in the Quran that you don't do charity to draw attention to what you are doing. You know, most of them aren't doing terrorist stuff. Charity in secret is known to God, and that's what matters. So wearing a disguise or mask to hide your identity from people, so you don't get credit for doing it, is quite acceptable to them and they understand it. That's where you see the people at the mosque. The different groups wear these things. That's where it comes from.
> NF: You must feel good when you think about all of that.
> Than: It does make you feel good. People say what makes you the proudest is when you put a loaf of bread in someone's hand and they look up with sometimes tears in their eyes and say that they haven't had a loaf of bread all to themselves in years.

I could tell Thanatos was emotional. But although we were together for a few hours, he hadn't told me about his morning yet. He'd had a funeral to attend. An older man, whose wife died a couple of months ago, just let himself go. Thanatos helped the man's social worker to get a funeral together and a proper grave.

"Sometimes the only thing I can do is get them buried so that there is a marker there. And someone will come by and they may not know the person, but they will know a person is there. He is close to his wife now."

The man representing death recalled a few events, including the death of a young woman who was eight and a half months pregnant. She was prostituting. She and others would climb over a razor wire and get up on a roof to smoke crack. One night she tried to climb up, and she fell three storeys to the asphalt and died along with her baby.

"I was in contact with her social worker and all she had for the baby was a DVD of the animated movie Anastasia. The autopsy proved that the baby was a girl. They allowed the baby to be buried separately. They gave her a permit and filled out a stillbirth rather than a fetus because it was close enough to nine months and developed far enough that they put it as an enforced stillbirth, so we got her buried up in Mountain View, and she's got a little marker there and it just says 'Elizabeth and her daughter Anastasia.'"

It takes a lot to be able to be in that area all the time, facing danger, saving lives of many people who will not change, but also helping others whose lives will never be the same.

"Fourteen people died with my business card on them," said Thanatos.

Looking at his eyes reflecting so much sadness, I could see how much strength he has, as a human being, as a friend, as a family man. "You are a strong man," I told him.

"I try. I cry for these people sometimes. I cry over some of the things I've seen. I just do what I can."

"Having emotions is just normal."

"It's when it doesn't happen that you worry. If it didn't affect me emotionally, I would wonder what I was doing. My wife said the same thing. You do what you can. You keep them alive ... one day at a time."

6

PHOENIX JONES — PART I

My adventure took an unexpected turn when I met with Phoenix Jones, the most solicited Real Life Super Hero.

After taking the bus from Vancouver, British Columbia, crossing the border, and finally arriving in Seattle, Washington, I took a cab to my hotel room and took some time to relax. I had an appointment with Phoenix Jones a little later that evening.

Since my schedule had changed, and I wanted to make sure to be able to get a hold of PJ, I asked Peter for the superhero's phone number in case I needed to contact him. The answer was clear: No. Some journalists had gotten PJ's phone number in the past, and his phone rang all the time. I told him I wouldn't share it with anyone, but the answer was firm.

At first, getting to know the community was like being a detective: find out who's good and who's not; find out who's there for the attention, and who's there to really make a difference. Who likes drama, who's honest, and who's a hypocrite? Because of Facebook, I was able to read over 130 RLSH's profiles every day, and follow every status, every comment, every response, every opinion, and every opposition. But to really be accepted as a journalist, I had to have someone back me up.

That day Thanatos, who is, as I said, one of the most respected men in the community, posted the video of us on YouTube and on his blog, stating, "Meeting with Nadia Fezzani today at Mountain View Cemetery. If anyone gets the opportunity to talk with her, you will find her honest and really deeply and positively interested in what we do and why." Then it seemed like having the approval of "Death" made people feel better about accepting me.

I was in my hotel room when the phone rang. It was Phoenix Jones.

I'd been looking forward to meeting him for a few months now, and I was interested to see if he was as I had imagined. I knew he was a mixed martial arts champion, and that he also practised tae kwon do, wrestling, and karate.

He was downstairs, standing in front of the hotel lobby couches when I first saw him. He wore full gear without his mask, and he appeared to be in fighting form. He was accompanied by a beautiful woman, whom I recognized.

"Hey, Nadia!" he said, while shaking my hand. "This is my wife, Purple Reign." As we approached the couch, he told me that he had brought his equipment and we were going straight to patrol, where I would meet the other guys. He looked just like I remembered him from TV. It wasn't like seeing an actor in a movie and then being disappointed when we see what they really look like in person. Phoenix Jones is six feet tall with a very athletic build. Purple looked to be in good shape, too, with a shorter frame, a beautiful face, and very long, straight purple hair. They were engaged, but they called each other husband and wife.

As we talked about our schedule, I could feel people looking at Phoenix. PJ was showing me his mini-microphones and hearing system, the kind security guards have around their wrists and in their ears to communicate with each other.

"The ear piece and the front microphone go straight to the camera guy that we have with us," explained PJ. "It records all of the talking that we do, with the videos, the entire night. So if there's an event where the police have to intervene, we give them the videos and the recorded audio, the guy's face, and us detaining him. The video is admissible in court."

PJ showed me his tactical gear, everything from the bulletproof vest, protective mask, leg trauma plates, and ballistic cup, to the taser, pepper spray, collapsible baton, and so on. He also carried a tracking system to show people where he is, his attorney's business card, a camera that stays on his chest, and a LAN cable that connects to his iPhone to send videos to the police, among many other things. He was explaining that when Purple doesn't patrol, she writes police reports from home that get transferred to his phone.

A man and a woman, dressed to go out, approached us, and the man offered his business card to the RLSH. He introduced himself as a lawyer and offered his services, but PJ gently declined, as he already had his lawyer. Once the lawyer was gone, PJ explained to me that many people want to represent him because he's been getting lots of publicity. He added that the law firm he works with "represents the un-representable. And I thought that was kind of weird, because I don't do anything illegal. If five steps is illegal, then I go four and a half."

But PJ doesn't only fight crime. He is also able to help people who are in a critical situation. That's where his training comes in handy: first aid, CPR, nurse's delegation course training, first responder training, community emergency response training, crisis management, and de-escalation tactics. I'll stop here, but the list is longer.

PJ and Purple were going over a booklet that shows the crimes in the city and looking at their patrol logs. They were showing me the maps indicating how many types of different assaults had occurred in the "bad" areas — where we were going to patrol. Eight women had been attacked in a specific area, and PJ explained how important it was for him to patrol as much as possible. "If you're not doing 15 hours a week, you are not going to win because criminals are putting their life into this. And I don't like to lose."

He went on: "As you find all these other superheroes, you are going to find out that balancing their life is very difficult. Most people end up having to slack in one area and it will have to be superheroing, because they have families and other stuff to do. My family and I, this is what we do. We do superheroing. We do it together. If you don't have a job, you can't be a professional superhero because you can't buy your own stuff. If you don't have a girlfriend or wife who trusts you and knows that you are out there fighting crime, you are not going to survive. If you don't have bulletproof gear, you are not going to survive. If my wife didn't find out where all the crime is in the city and tell me where to go, I would not even find crime. I used to walk around the city five hours a night and I would find no incident."

Tonight, we knew exactly where to go. I was ready to leave the hotel, already wearing my bulletproof vest. A car was waiting for us outside. As I was invited to get in, I saw a young man in his 20s in the driver's seat, not wearing any gear. "Hi, I'm Ryan McNamee," he said, looking at me through his glasses. The tall, baby-faced, brown-haired man is the one who records each and every patrol with the Rain City Superhero Movement, Phoenix Jones's group. He was also filming when Phoenix Jones had the pepper-spray adventure, and McNamee had received a few punches himself from the bad guys.

As we got in the car and began driving to the destination, PJ did something I didn't expect. But first, he explained why.

"The guys who are on my team need to look up to me and know that nobody can hurt me. When I get out there, I have to be somebody who's totally different. I think that's what makes a great leader compared to just regular people: leaders know the presentation is necessary. There has to be more of the seriousness; it's about getting the job done, motivate the others to get the job done and understand where the energy needs to be. When we had our conversation earlier, it was very personable and an easy sit-down conversation. You are going to see a very different side of me when we patrol. That is necessary to complete the mission. So beforehand I always do something to have a little fun because it becomes a lonely place sometimes. I listen to music and think about the rules of engagement and what would be the right thing in certain scenarios."

He turned the music up loud. Rihanna's song "We Found Love" was playing, and PJ started singing out loud and dancing in the front passenger seat, getting pumped up by the song. I couldn't hide the huge smile on my face when I heard him singing along with Rihanna with his not very melodic voice. I had to record him. He reminded me of a kid who was just about to get a huge surprise. That said, the mood quickly changed when we got out of the car.

We parked and met up with five of PJ's crew. In my blue jeans, I didn't quite fit in with the team. Everybody else was in full black gear, with different styles, except for Phoenix who was in black and gold, and El Caballero with his gold *luchador* mask — usually used for wrestling, especially in Mexico — and a purple vest underneath his black leather coat. They all had either military or mixed martial arts backgrounds. They all had their faces covered. It was getting colder, and Purple offered me her purple coat, which I couldn't refuse, as she had a black one for herself.

After we were all introduced, PJ explained to me that there are different positions on the team. One person goes in first when there is an issue. He assesses the situation. If he draws his weapon, everybody else draws their weapons. The first person is the leader and sets the example. If anything goes wrong, it's his fault. That task is usually given to PJ or to Pitch Black. When there are enough people, like today, they form two teams. The second man is the backup. If there is only one team, Pitch Black will be PJ's backup. If there are two teams, the Mantis or El Caballero will be the backup. They are right there to protect the leader. The third one is a "floater," there to protect Purple while she's on the phone and can't focus on her surroundings. That person makes sure that no one else enters the fights. Purple's jobs are to hang back and call 9-1-1 if it becomes necessary, and to get the vehicle if they need to leave the situation.

PJ assigned me a position: "You stay with Purple and make sure no one comes and tries to sneak up behind her. And she's got your back, too, to make sure that no one goes behind your back or tries to sneak up behind you."

If PJ runs off and Purple cannot see him, she can still hear him because of the earpiece.

"So when that happens," said PJ, "it's important that you don't talk to her. If the incident takes place close by, then it's her job to get away so that she can get good accurate information."

Purple elaborated, "Normally, when there's a big fight right in front of me, I can't call 9-1-1, so I take the position of standing across the alleyway or across the street. There, I can see everything and the camera is recording. I make sure that if there's any injury, we get an ambulance."

PJ was not happy about his gear. The charges had been dropped, but the authorities kept his gear anyway. Thankfully, PJ had an older version of the same gear for the upper body. In the meantime, he was simply wearing black pants while patrolling.

"In my other boots, the ones the police stole from me when I was arrested, I had a GPS tracker," added PJ. "So if I was lost on the street, Purple could literally track me down and help me."

Before leaving on patrol, PJ said we should take a picture all together. He put me in the middle of the team, and we got on top of the barricade that separated us from the water. Ryan didn't quite like the result of his picture and asked us to step down and take another shot, in a rank position forming a V, with me in front of it all (at PJ's request). It felt like a great memory in the making.

Purple explained to me that we were going to walk through the crowds and intervene in any fights that we saw. We'd call cabs for people who were drunk. And we'd go into an area with a lot of drug-related violence. When all of the bars closed for the night and everybody was gone, we would patrol more of the drug areas.

We reached an area that PJ's team frequently patrolled, but the police were already there.

"Since the cops finally showed up to do their job," said PJ, "we are going to move on to the next place."

PJ had Purple and the Mantis stay with me at all times, for my protection. People were looking at us. When we arrived on the main strip, it was worse. We could barely walk a block without someone throwing themselves at Phoenix Jones, for the good things or the bad. Some girls were screaming with excitement; others were polite and just smiling. Some asked for autographs, but more often they wanted to take a picture with PJ. The rest of the group didn't seem as interesting to the public. Once in a while someone would ask for a picture with the group. The teammates seemed to be very used to this; when PJ was asked for a picture, they would just wait a little farther on until it was all over. Then it started again.

Some men on the street threatened PJ. "You wanna fight? Huh? Pfffff … Phoenix Jones!" with voices full of anger. But the threats weren't really scary, even if sometimes the guys were beefy. It was bizarre to see how people's appreciation could interfere with PJ's task. He might be watching a verbal fight in case it turned into a physical fight, and people were bugging him for a picture, even those who didn't know who he was, asking, "Are you a superhero?" The team told me that sometimes people get right in the middle of a situation, just asking for a picture, making it harder for the Real Life Super Heroes to achieve their objective.

So far, aside from a couple of fights, the night was pretty calm. When a situation did arise, it was hard for the Mantis and Purple to stay with me constantly, so only one would stay. I told them not to worry about me, but since PJ received hostile criticism from Real Life Super Heroes and the media when the pepper-spray story occurred, he wanted to make sure nothing like that would happen again, and he wanted me protected. I explained to PJ that I didn't care about what other people were saying and that I was fully aware of the risks. I didn't need extra protection; being with them was good enough for me. PJ recounted an event where an American journalist was with them when they faced a gunman. The journalist was apparently shocked and just wanted to leave and never come back. I told him I was not that person, and I wondered why such a person would embed himself with RLSHs.

The Mantis and I had the opportunity to talk a lot about superheroes and many unrelated things. He let me know he was recently in trouble with PJ for getting a tattoo of the Rain City Superhero Movement on his shoulder. PJ was not happy, telling him it was not the right way to maintain anonymity.

We patrolled from 11 p.m. until around 4 a.m., and nothing major happened. Sometimes we split the superhero group in two and walked on opposite sides of the street.

Some people might say PJ is arrogant, and I could see how he rubs many in the RLSH community the wrong way. He often talks about himself and his achievements. But on the other hand, he has a self-deprecating sense of humour, so perhaps it's just his way.

On our way back to the car, PJ wanted to show me the worst area of the city, a place, it is said, even many police officers avoid. As we walked through an open parking lot, PJ told Midnight Jack to give me his taser, "just in case." I had never held one in my hands. I was hoping it wasn't like pepper spray, where the risks of hurting yourself are high.

We walked toward a nightclub PJ wanted to pass. There were a few men out front scowling at us. Two men crossed the street to avoid us, saying, "You guys look goofy," in an insulting tone. PJ crossed the street to talk to them. "We might look goofy," he told them, "but if you're in trouble, we'll be there to defend you." And the guys' attitudes changed. We all went to join them, and PJ and the two men were talking, smiling, and laughing in a friendly way. We made our way to the cars, to call it a night.

I was a little disappointed that I didn't get the chance to see how PJ and his team intervene. On the other hand, it's nice when it's peaceful. I still had a couple more nights to patrol with the Rain City Superhero Movement.

⚡

We were just about to get into our cars when we noticed a man acting suspiciously near a parked car. He was fiddling with his keys, and something seemed off. When the man noticed us watching him, he started walking away. Phoenix and the team regrouped. PJ asked three teammates to take off their masks (so the stranger wouldn't be afraid), and told them to ask the man if he was okay and what was going on. The man looked behind and saw the unmasked superheroes following him. He hailed a taxi and hopped in. Over the microphones, the team was communicating, and the superheroes near the cab told Phoenix the man was leaving. We ran up the hill and got there in time to stop the driver. A superhero explained to the taxi driver that his customer had done something questionable and we wanted to ask him about it. The driver didn't want any trouble, so he asked the passenger to get out. We asked the man what he had been doing with that car. He said it was his and that he was trying to get in, but he had decided to get a cab instead since he was drunk.

The superheroes were calm with the man, except for the Mantis who was agitated and impatient. Phoenix Jones told him to calm down. I was actually very impressed by Phoenix Jones's patience. The man wasn't giving straight answers, so the team asked him to go back to the car and show us that it was really his. This time he was able to unlock the door. "See? I told you it was my car!" said the man. "Hey, no problem, man. But we had to verify," PJ said.

As we were finishing up with the man, I looked behind me and saw a tall black man talking with Purple and two other superheroes. There was something about him — it wasn't just his sloppy look, his large pants, or his unsmiling face. He seemed agitated. Something about him didn't feel right. At first, he was being creepy and impolite, staring at Purple's body. Then he looked at Midnight Jack and asked, "Hey, what's up? Are you one of those superheroes?" After hearing an affirmative answer, the guy became all nice. Then he asked, "Where is your leader?"

Purple told the guys not to answer, but it was too late: El Caballero (often called "El Cabby") and Midnight Jack pointed toward Phoenix. The man drew a gun and waved it around. Purple immediately talked into the microphone. "Signal 4," she said, which means the individual has a deadly weapon and the superheroes are the intended target.

The Mantis, maybe because of lack of experience, yelled: "He has a gun! He has a gun!" instead of following protocol and keeping quiet.

The gunman said, "I'm gonna kill that motherfucker."

I didn't have any way to hear Purple's warning, as I wasn't connected to their audio system, but I saw the man walking toward me, with one of his hands in his pants. I was picking up very negative vibes, so I turned around and told PJ that the man was coming. The guy's face displayed hostility and aggression. I wanted to get away from the sidewalk, to get out of his way, but because of a car parked along the road, I was stuck between the car and a viaduct wall. The guy passed beside me with barely a couple of inches between us. As he got closer to PJ, I rushed away to join the group members farther away.

The guy made a few comments to PJ, who responded in a tone that showed he wasn't afraid, and then the gunman crossed the street away from us. The superheroes who had been standing by PJ rushed over to be with us, and the owner of the car came with us as well, as PJ didn't want him to be alone. We heard a *click* as the gunman chambered a round. He was prepared to shoot.

Phoenix didn't want anything to happen to any of us. So we stayed in areas with good cover, like the alleys between buildings. We were still tracking the gunman. Rather than following him, however, we were walking in front him. As he approached, we would move ahead. Purple and the Mantis called the authorities, as was their task. We waited. And waited.

Instead of being afraid, I wanted to go talk to the gunman. El Caballero felt the same. It was the adrenalin rush that was making us feel brave. But Phoenix objected to our idea. He reminded us that a bulletproof vest did not give absolute protection and that it wasn't safe to do something like that. We kept moving ahead of the gunman while keeping an eye on him. The man from the car was excited to be with us and kept saying, "This is so exciting! I'm so glad I didn't take the cab!" Finally, the police arrived about six minutes later. But it was too late. The man had vanished into the night.

PJ wasn't happy. He requested the team all meet in a specific parking lot. When we arrived there, the white concrete building was empty. The team all parked their cars in the same area and got out to meet. I didn't want to interfere with the others or make them feel uncomfortable, so I stayed in the car. I could tell that PJ was giving them trouble for the mistakes a few of them had made, especially providing information about Phoenix Jones's location to the gunman without knowing what he wanted or who he was.

The result of the meeting was that everyone was suspended, PJ included. "If I die, I want to die because someone got me; not because of my guys!" he said. "Does that make sense? I can teach a procedure, I can teach you how to use your microphone, but I can't teach common sense. So everyone here is suspended, including me, because we have to figure out what we're going to do. But if they ask 'where's your leader?' don't tell them. It's about common sense. And you are so street-smart that I'm not sure why you would do that."

It was after 6 a.m. Although not all of the team members had day jobs, a few of them did. When everyone was back in their cars, PJ and Purple drove me back to the hotel. I invited them in to the sitting area in my room, and they sat down to debrief the night's events.

We went over what had happened. PJ thought the gunman was the friend of a coke dealer who had been busted a week ago because of PJ. Phoenix thought he had seen them together in the past. But the reality is that we'll never know. After that event, however, Jones was thinking about patrolling on his own again. He repeated, "If I die, I want to die because someone got me. Not because of my guys." He was very disappointed that his teammates had told the gunman about his whereabouts. Since Midnight

Jack used to be a criminal, Phoenix figured that he should have known better and not said anything. In spite of problems, Phoenix was not ready to quit.

⚡

Jones is very careful about who he lets into his personal life. According to him, only one journalist had ever been to his place, and only because Jones was moving out. He didn't give his phone number to the media anymore and he didn't share his private life with others. When he told me that, I wasn't quite sure whether to believe him or not — he *had* given me his phone number, making me promise not to give it to anyone. I realized he was telling the truth once he brought me to his home for a meeting. As I entered his apartment, his teammates all stopped talking at once, looking confused.

"Huh.... We're not wearing our masks, PJ," said one of them.

PJ was reassuring. "She's fine. Don't worry. You can tell her whatever you want."

Some guys seemed a little uncomfortable at first, but they soon changed their minds and welcomed me to the group.

Jones was still upset with their performance from the previous night.

We all met in the living room to discuss what had happened. I noticed a funny thing: most of them wore the same shoes they wore during patrol (but not PJ and Purple). Some shoes are easy to recognize. While PJ told everyone about what he thought should or should not have been done, people shared thoughts on how to act the next time something similar happened. The meeting ended on a positive note, and we had a conversation about patrolling, media relations, and how to talk in front of a camera. I have to say, Phoenix Jones does not look intimidated when he's on TV, but at 23 years old, he didn't care much about what people thought about his public comments. He likes to call things the way he sees them, no matter the cost. I gave him some tips about appearance and responses in the media, not knowing if he would follow them or not; although, he did seem to appreciate my media relations input.

Phoenix had no free time that day, so I took the opportunity to interview four of the other team members. There was Ryan, the photographer/videographer; the Mantis, the tall and slim one; quiet Nameless;

and skinny and energetic Midnight Jack. As we all sat around the table, I offered something to drink and we started talking about the world of Real Life Super Heroes.

While chatting, Midnight Jack explained that, before becoming a RLSH, just like the Mantis, he saw PJ on the news and thought helping people was an amazing thing to do. Midnight Jack thought about it for a week and decided to patrol on his own, then he went with another team. A few months later, he met other RLSHs and decided to join up with PJ.

I wanted to know more about their motives, so we started to talk about their pasts. Midnight Jack opened up to say that before he started patrolling, he'd had a lot of bad times in his life — selling drugs, beating people up for money they owed him. Hitting rock bottom, he saw himself as a bad person and he decided to get clean.

"I wanted sort of penance or some community service where I could give back to the community. I would help other ways if I knew how, but this is what I'm good at," said Jack. "I did a lot of bad things and this is my positive contribution: to help rebuild the community that I helped destroy. I work really hard on helping people who are down on their luck and don't have a person to turn to. They can turn to me."

Nameless was emotionally abused by his father, and verbally and physically abused by many members of his family. His half-brother, who was a couple of years older than him, tried to kill Nameless twice. The first time, he tried to drown him in the Columbia River while on a family vacation. The second time, they had been play-fighting and Nameless "got him good." His half-brother got really angry, and Nameless's mother had to step in when his brother was bashing him with a club. All Nameless wanted was to be friends with his half-brother. But that brother wanted to spend more time with his own older brother, who was living with his "crack whore" mom, as Nameless describes it. The future RLSH was also bullied at school, beaten up by other teens. He chose not to fight back violently. Today he fights back in other ways.

For his part, the Mantis explained that his parents were both drug addicts. He lived with his father in the back of a truck, on a reservation, on the beach, in a tent, all in extreme poverty. His mother was incarcerated for four years for armed robbery and possession of cocaine. The Mantis was only four years old when his mother went to prison. She was a pathological liar. At eight, his mother requested him for a couple of weeks to introduce him to his new stepfather, who was physically abusive.

He recalled, "I had to babysit my mom a lot, as she was in abusive relationships. It was constantly a choice of drugs over children, liquor over children, and men over children. My sisters don't talk to her anymore. I always had a Nintendo, but I never had the attention or affection. I was raised by my friends."

The Mantis recalled when he was about four or five and his older sister took him out of the house. She later told him that when they went back to the house, their mother was sitting on their couch, nodding off with a needle in her arm.

"My mom was in a relationship with a man who beat her to unconsciousness," the Mantis went on. "Back when I was four, I called the police and said: 'My mom is sleeping because of what he did.' They came really fast. Many years later, when I was about 16, she broke up with her boyfriend, but she had left some of her mom's jewellery that was irreplaceable to her at his house. So we showed up at his place, in a rural area. He was being super nice and everything was going really well. We took some iced tea, and then he grabbed her hair, and he pulled out a knife, and he was trying to cut her throat. She was pushing with both of her hands against his arms. I didn't know what to do. I grabbed his .22 rifle that was sitting in the room next to where they were. I didn't know if it was loaded — I just reacted. I shot him in the neck. He was still alive. I heard a few days later that he had died. I was totally under the assumption that I took his life. I couldn't sleep, I couldn't eat, I had gastritis. I had ulcers in my stomach because I was just so stressed out about this. It got so bad! The police came to me and told me that he died of a cocaine overdose. I believe they were lying; I think this is how my brain deals with the shock of what happened. I lived with that my entire life. I stopped him from living. But I remembered one thing that really made it okay: when my mom came to me and gave me a big hug, saying, 'Thank you for saving my life.' It took me years before I could talk about it. From the police and hospital, his family and my family, there was no negative response. I took it on myself to bring the negativity. But I shot somebody because he was going to kill my mother. It messed with me a lot. So it might not be the entire reason why I started doing this, but this is one of the things that made me the person I am today."

Midnight Jack also had parental problems, although not as dramatic as some of his colleagues' family situations. Aside from saying that his stepfather was an asshole, he mentioned that his father wasn't around until he turned 20. He always felt unwanted by his parents. But what kept him going were comic books.

Nameless then talked about times he remembered when he separated fights and used words to make the fighters feel guilty and sometimes even cry. But he also learned that it can be hard to control his emotions, especially when patrolling alone, which he has done a few times. He recalled one night, a long time ago, when "a guy had shoved a girl against a wall. He was struggling, ripping at her clothes," in an alley. Nameless lost it. He grabbed the aggressor, kicked him, and "slammed his head into the wall and he crumbled. And he didn't get back up."

We continued the discussion talking about police officers and how it's hard sometimes even for them to treat people with respect, regardless of the crime they have committed.

However, just like the police, superheroes have a code of conduct to follow if they want to be respected by the RLSH community. Even when situations are frustrating, they have to be in control and do what's right.

Midnight Jack whispered, "Like the guy who peed on Phoenix." Yes, even when they get peed on.

Nameless recalled a couple of nights when people did mean things to the Seattle superheroes. "I actually had to restrain Jack once," said Nameless. "I've had to pull Ghost off of someone. I have had to stop Pitch. I, myself, have had to be stopped once by Phoenix. I had to pull Phoenix once. Everyone is kind of checking for each other."

I had to ask if that meant they were vigilantes more than superheroes. Vigilantes make their own justice, they do not obey the law, and they want to harm those who are in the wrong. Midnight Jack didn't want to talk too much about his darker days, but he admitted that he had beaten up a date rapist "pretty good" behind a nightclub. "But that was before Midnight Jack. When you put the mask on, you can't do vigilante justice. We need to hold ourselves to a very high standard with the mask. We need to operate inside of the confines of the law."

A moment later, Phoenix called me and said that if I wanted to feel like a Real Life Super Hero and be treated like everyone else, I had to wear a mask. We drove to a costume shop. I wanted a red one, masquerade style. I chose the most standard one. Phoenix Jones bought it. I wanted to pay him back. He refused. Later on, I hid the money in one of his coat pockets.

We then went to visit his lawyer, Caitlin. I had the opportunity to chat with her after her meeting with PJ, and I found out that PJ always had her services pro bono. Caitlin recounted memories of when she introduced her Marvel and Captain America author friends to PJ at a comic convention. They were asking about his gear and PJ had tased himself in the chest to show them what it does. "You could see sparks!" she said. People were speechless. After chatting for about a half hour, I thanked her for confirming certain facts regarding PJ and we were on our way.

Tonight the team was undergoing a special training session. PJ decided that it was time for testing the guys' physical capacities. Each had an appointment, except Purple, who was at home with her son. At 8 p.m. we waited for them at Green Lake in a large and beautiful park, lit up by city lights. PJ and I were the first ones to arrive, and we discussed the purpose of the night's training. But then, we waited. And waited. And the team members didn't show up. Phoenix, impatient, called them. Some were lost; another had no money for gas and was trying to find a way to get there. In other words, they all had excuses. I saw a little bit of Phoenix in this, as he was sometimes late for interviews and appointments. But tonight, no one was on time. We were freezing outside, waiting, until finally, about an hour after we had arrived, all the cars showed up within about 15 minutes of each other.

Phoenix said they needed to be training more and wanted to see who could run around the lake and come back within a specific time frame. PJ asked me to participate as well. Ryan — the photographer/videographer — and I ran together, taking walking breaks at times. After about 20 minutes, we got back to the starting line last … or almost. One superhero who had just come back from a trip and wasn't with us the previous night couldn't keep up. The leader told him he could not patrol until he proved he could run and be in good shape.

The Mantis asked for money for gas, as he wasn't working. His wife supported him in his project to be a Real Life Super Hero and was taking care of everything, but right now they were just broke. PJ gave him some money for gas and then gave money to someone else as well. The night was over.

⚡

The next day, PJ picked me up and brought me to the Dreaming, a comic book store where he gets his correspondence and material delivered. I had seen a video about this place on CNN. The CNN story began on the street, where a man named Dan had witnessed someone trying to steal his car. He was calling 9-1-1 when he saw Phoenix Jones running after the thief. In the video, PJ was shown going into the Dreaming, entering the secret room dressed as a civilian, and coming out with his full gear on. Back outside he was able to meet with Dan and described everything he was carrying: taser, night stick, mace/tear gas, bulletproof vest, and stab plates.*

As we entered the store, he introduced me to the owner, Aaron, and the manager, a woman known as "J."

> PJ: This place was across from where I actually got my haircut. I started talking with Aaron and told him I had this idea: I wanted to walk around dressed up like a comic book character and beat up criminals. He probably thought I was kidding and just left it alone, but next time I came in, we sat down with a couple of other guys in the room, including a medic, and he asked me if I was serious. I said yes. He said, "Okay, there are a few things that I think you should do." And we had this long conversation.
>
> Aaron: It was perfect that someone with a police training background just happened to be there as well. He knew the right resources.
>
> PJ: We talked about martial arts and came down to the fact that I needed to get a lot of things, including a bulletproof vest. I had never even been shot at and I didn't think I was going to need it. Aaron said, "Dude, for what it's going to cost you!"

---

* "Real Life Super Hero Stops Crime," YouTube video, 1:24, from CNN newscast, posted by "niza310," January 4, 2011, https://youtu.be/sJQi7yYhVVA.

The friend who was with them was a retired police officer. He went to his car and got PJ a bulletproof vest.

> PJ: The next day on patrol, I got shot. So I came in here the next day and I had this huge blood blister and broken ribs. It was terrible! I told Aaron, "Dude, I am sold! Thank you!" Because otherwise, I would be dead. And that was the end of this blue spandex crap. It was just a pair of fighting shorts, boxing gloves, no protective armour, a little fedora hat, and a sock that I had cut in the middle and tied across my face. It was straight-up stupid. You live and you learn.
>
> Aaron: We didn't realize that we were going to hide his identity at that point. [Turning toward Jones] I don't even think the medic and the retired police officer would remember that they have seen you without the mask until later.
>
> PJ: It was such a random day for them, but for me it changed my life.

Then Aaron recounted the day when PJ came in the store, just after being shot. Aaron didn't see the wound itself, but he saw the bandages and the bruises that had spread.

"Imagine if someone throws paint on you; it had blood drips, but inside my body," said PJ. "It was like the weirdest thing, but I guess that's what front trauma bleeding looks like."

At the time that happened, PJ didn't think he would continue. Aaron told him he had a feeling PJ would not stop. And he was right. The shop owner imagined that many people would be looking for the masked crusader, so he offered to keep his mail. Later, as his media requests increased, PJ would hide behind a door in the store and emerge for dramatic effect.

"And there were times where he would actually change back," J recalled. "He had his own Superman phone booth."

PJ added that sometimes when his car was far away, he would come in the store to change out of his superhero gear after busting up a crime, but he hardly ever used the backroom. In fact, he brought me to where the secret room was hidden by a rack of books, just like the rest of the walls in the entire store. He opened the door and showed me what was inside: miscellaneous objects and things to clean up the store. It was a utility closet.

⚡

Next we went to the Central Police Station in Seattle to meet with the Street Robbery and Homicide Director. Though PJ's identity had already been revealed in the media, he still wore his superhero suit. I asked why, and he said it was to keep his image. To maintain my anonymity, I wore my red mask. After the security check, the receptionist called the director who did not make us wait. The director was very welcoming and courteous, and our conversation started as we waited for the elevator. A few people crossed our path and saluted us. But the funniest part was when a man told PJ he had to see something in a specific office. It was the office of a lieutenant, who was sitting at his desk when we arrived. He saluted us. On his left was a bookshelf, holding a picture frame of Phoenix Jones's team, with one member's face cut out and replaced with the picture of the lieutenant. Clearly not all of the cops felt antagonistic toward PJ. Everybody had a good laugh. A couple people approached us and asked if they could take pictures with Phoenix Jones. PJ gave the director files with pictures, names, and descriptions of the members of his team for validation purposes — apparently some people patrolled the streets saying they were in PJ's team when it was untrue.

We then went to pick up Purple, and PJ took me to his mother's place where he grew up. I met his adoptive mother. We sat down in the living room, accompanied by an autistic boy whom PJ's mother was fostering. The living room was filled with Phoenix Jones's trophies and medals from martial arts to baseball to bowling. I could tell his mother was very proud of him. We stayed a bit to chat, and she confirmed many things PJ had told me about his past. I felt gratitude again, that a superhero would bring me to his parents' place.

I took a break at the hotel before another team meeting at PJ's home. When I arrived, the Mantis was waiting for me with a surprise: his mask.

His green-and-black Zorro-type mask with a big M visible in the middle. He wanted to give it to me. I was told that in the RLSH world, it means a lot. It means that person really respects you. I kept his mask with my mask from Superheroes Anonymous. His wife had also cut me a triangle of red fabric to help me hide my face.

Although we were in Seattle, it was still December, and it was very cold at night. Since my regular coat was fitted, I was not able to close it over a bulletproof vest. So I went to a second-hand store and got a very nice washable black jacket that looked like new ... for $5!

I had the defensive flashlight that had been given to me by Death's Head Moth, my bulletproof vest, and my new red mask. I was ready for patrol. We saw a woman being held against her will on a street where not many people were walking by. She was obviously afraid, trapped against a building wall by the body and arms of a man who kept her there. Nothing else was happening, and he was just talking to her, so PJ decided to stick around to see if the situation escalated. We stayed there for about 15 minutes, during which the man became more and more agitated. The woman was crying and the man became more threatening. Someone from the team called 9-1-1, and the man was arrested.

Another incident also involved a woman. As we were walking the streets, we saw her crying. She was partly hidden by the smoke of a hot dog cart, and by the nightclubs. Purple, normally the only woman on the team, is usually the one who approaches women in distress. The team agreed that this made the women feel more comfortable when they were approached. However, this woman refused any type of help.

Tonight, we were going to be part of a documentary. A TV crew from Sweden was coming to film us. I didn't think I should be in the documentary, but PJ told me I was his recruit, and I had to do exactly like everyone else.

The TV crew met us downtown around 11 p.m. We parked in the area where the team usually patrols. Q, a soldier, was waiting for us there. He had mini-cameras for every superhero on the team. Each person taped a camera to their chest. That way, everything would be recorded and no false accusations could be made. That had been a problem for PJ's crew in the past when a rival superhero concocted allegations of misconduct against the team.

It was cold with a light rain, but that didn't stop anyone from being motivated to patrol. As the film crew arrived, I was introduced as the rookie.
PJ explained to the interviewer that I had just started and that I didn't have
much experience. After interviewing a few people on the team, the media
team turned to me. They asked me about the feeling of patrolling, my
motivations, and other little questions. I couldn't answer some questions,
as I didn't have enough experience to actually have a response, but I spoke
truthfully, mentioning everything from the martial arts classes I had taken
to other experiences I have that are beneficial to such a task. They asked me
if having a woman on the team was important. I said yes, because a woman
in need of help might not feel comfortable being approached by a man.

The crew filmed us patrolling on opposite sides of the street and together. There were a few incidents, but nothing as extreme as the first
day: fights of different kinds; people asking for autographs. But I felt that
having the cameras there cleared the streets. The "bad" people didn't want
to be filmed. As we walked, we could see many people just going away.
The other superheroes didn't quite get the same attention from the camera
as PJ. But then again, they didn't necessarily want it, and some of them
intentionally avoided it.

Although nothing extreme happened that night, those hours were still
special to me. The most interesting part was the feeling I had on patrol.
Putting the gear on gave me a feeling of power and confidence that I hadn't
experienced before. I was walking very straight and noticing every little
detail around me, looking everywhere, seeing everything: walkers, bystanders, emotions on faces, activities. It's like I had eyes all around my head. I
was more alert to my senses and could hear the noise more than usual. I
was ready to defend whomever, no matter what.

7

CALIFORNIA

N ever has a Real Life Super Hero been more aptly named. Motor Mouth was already talking a mile a minute when he picked me up at my hotel.

I wasn't going to have as much time with the leader of the Pacific Protectorate as I'd had with the other teams since I was visiting the California Initiative in San Francisco that weekend. I tried to be careful about the way I broached the topic, as there is tension between both teams. I was going to spend two days with each.

His bleach-blond hair looked exactly like in his pictures. But back when the photos were taken, he had been carrying his 160 pounds mostly in his belly. Since then he had gained some weight — he was now around 215 pounds — and he kept telling me he had to work it out. He was shorter than I expected, being only 5'6". Nonetheless, he had the stature and posture of a man who should not be underestimated.

He wasn't dressed in his black superhero uniform or the black ski mask that covers his lower face. He didn't even have the black leather jacket he often wears over his black bulletproof vest. Today he was just a normal guy; a substitute teacher who works with young people with cognitive disabilities.

"Oh, I have been punched in the face before," said Motor Mouth. "I actually have scars I can show you on my hands and my arms. I have had kids cut me with sharp pencils. I've had children who tried to bite me. I actually have bite mark scars on my left hand," he said as he showed me the scars.

Then he told me about a friend of his who was working with a class: "A 14-year-old student was trying to pick a fight with a much smaller eight-year-old student. The teacher was trying to break up the fight, and she stepped in the middle of the two boys, the same way I would on the street as a Real Life Super Hero. She told the student, 'You need to stop doing this.' The 14-year-old responded, 'Fuck you, bitch!' and he punched her in the throat. I heard the connection of skin just slap together. I picked the 14-year-old up, one arm underneath his arms, and one around his waist, and I ended up pinning him against the wall. It was not professional for me to do that, but at the same time I was afraid for the safety of my co-worker. I wasn't sure what was going to happen."

At that moment we were driving through a bad neighbourhood called Ghost Town. "People get shot and killed here," cautioned Motor Mouth.

"I took the kid down," he continued his story of the schoolyard incident. "We got him into a restraint and he started trying to bite me. At that point, other staff came running in and took over. It was a very scary experience, as I thought I was going to get fired. I had been there for almost two years at that point. But the administrator knew I was just trying to defend people."

He continued to explain his job: "Things will be really cool one second and then all of a sudden you have a student who will grab somebody by the hair. I saw a teenage student take out a boiling hot cup of noodles and throw it at another teacher. Luckily, the teacher saw it coming and she blocked it, but her whole arm got burned up. And they only make about nine dollars per hour.

"It makes for really good training for patrols!" he joked. "Through my job, I've also gotten my CPR certification, my basic first aid certification, and my AED training with the defibrillators."

We were on our way to pick up Motor Mouth's guys. Today we were going to patrol with two others: Cheshire Cat and Black Dawg. When we picked up Cheshire Cat, I was a little surprised to meet a proofreader in the e-book industry dressed in several tones of pink and purple — his leather jacket, his hair, and even his T-shirt, which included the image of a cat face. The only black clothing he wore were his pants and gloves. He was, indeed, representing the Cheshire Cat from *Alice's Adventures in Wonderland*. His face was covered in makeup of the same colours, done up in the face of a fiendish cat. Regardless of his colour selection, this flamboyant superhero was pretty intimidating — all 6'5" and 300 pounds of him. We introduced ourselves, and I have to admit I doubted he would be as active as Phoenix Jones on his patrols.

Cheshire Cat explained that his mandate was primarily homeless outreach, as well as providing first aid to those in need. "In Berkeley, we did some homeless outreach and there was a young lady who had some visible track marks on her arms. I'm not sure if she was doing heroin, but I know she was a user. Her marks were giving her pain. Obviously I can't cure her of that, but I gave her some small supplies and disinfected the wound. I said, 'Listen, I'm not going to judge you, but I'm going to at least try to get rid of the infection that you have going on right now.'"

Most superheroes have a specialty, and first aid is a common one among those who do not want to fight.

We arrived in Black Dawg's neighbourhood a few minutes later. I couldn't help but comment.

"This looks pretty bad!" I said, observing the dilapidated housing. "I would not walk alone around here."

Indeed, Motor Mouth confirmed it was an unsafe area.

We called Black Dawg, and he came out, all in black as his name suggests, with earrings in both ears and a shaved head. This security agent and music promoter was different from the other two. Though he was older (and shorter), he was in much better shape. During patrol Black Dawg covers his lower face with a piece of black fabric that has a white skull printed on it.

I was surprised that the Ray wasn't going to be with us. He had been a popular topic in the news and the community lately. I asked Motor Mouth where the Ray was, and he explained to me that after what had happened, and because he was drawing extremely negative attention, they had a meeting, and Motor Mouth was thinking of "benching him." And the Ray had only been with him for two months.

Motor Mouth (MM): The kid's got his heart in the right place, but his mind is too cluttered.

NF: So ... what happened?

MM: The first thing is with the Occupy Oakland event. There were violent protesters who were burning up dumpsters and breaking windows downtown. The Ray went down in full uniform, with his mask, homemade body armour and my shield that I let him borrow, and he went down there to protect the public. Everyone else on the team that night was busy, and the remainder of us had no way to get out of their personal obligations, like our jobs, college, and families. We told him to be prepared if he was going to go out there, as he had a moderately decent chance to engage with violent protesters or the cops.

From what I remember him telling me, he saw a couple running for their lives away from police officers in riot gear who had broken formation and were chasing them. The woman had fallen down on the ground, so the man tried to become a human shield. The police officer started beating them and the Ray stepped in with his shield so he could block him to let them get out of there. Then the cop went after him, so he struck the officer, and a number of officers came and started fighting the Ray. He ended up getting a sharp blow to the head and a sharp blow to the back. When he woke up, he was face down on the concrete, and there was blood all over him and all over the ground. His hands were cuffed behind his back. He ended up getting taken to a detention centre. And there was a veteran from the war in Iraq, and the police had beaten him so bad that he had a lacerated spleen and was spitting up blood. The Ray was the one that rallied the rest of the people in the detention area to go ahead and bring attention to the cause or get the cops to give the guy with a lacerated spleen leave for medical attention. So depending on how you look at it, the Ray indirectly ended up saving the guy's life. Then they took the Ray to Highland General

Hospital, handcuffed him down to a hospital gurney, and that's when he got stitches and everything.

NF: Did you ever help people during the Occupy?

MM: Yes. When the Oscar and Grant riots happened last year, we ended up rescuing a few businesses and we helped a young woman to get medical aid.

NF: Okay. Going back to the Ray, what is the second story?

Then Motor Mouth recalled having given an interview to the *San Francisco Weekly* newspaper with the Ray.

MM: The journalist was Lauren Smiley, and she had first come across as a very sympathetic voice to us, and we ended up giving her full access to what we do. From the perspective that she talked to the Ray and I, we thought it was going to be a very positive article. When the article came out, it was extremely negative toward the Ray. He didn't know how to talk to the media and she basically took advantage of that. He made comments which the average person would take as being very racist. For example, he spoke in reference to an altercation in a skateboard park where there was a number of African-American youths who were provoking others to fight. He said something like, 'There were so many black people there that it almost turned the day into night.' I'm sorry, but to me, that is an extremely racist statement. You can't say stuff like that. He made a lot of derogatory comments in there and he came off basically as a very ignorant boy or man-child from the suburbs that really was not worldly in the slightest, and had a very narrow black-and-white perspective on the world at large and was not altered at all. Due to a very sheltered background and a very ugly religious and military oriented family.

Personally, I respect him in the utmost and I support him 100 percent for what he did at Occupy Oakland, in the event that he did what he did because he was there to help the public and he was trying to protect people. He wasn't trying to be a problem for the cops, it just inadvertently came out that way from the perspective of the officers. We just think that because of some immaturity and a sense of unknown ignorance, his head was not in the right place for the article.

One of the problems RLSHs face is a lack of experience with media and public relations. It definitely seemed to be the case with Motor Mouth's young protege, the Ray.

⚡

As it was already evening, we went to a popular spot, and I don't think the superheroes could have chosen a better place to do surveillance. We walked to the intersection of two streets, which was home to a number of nightclubs. At night this area fills with young adults determined to party. On one of the corners, there were white four-foot-high cement blocks on an empty lot. We were surrounded by lights of many colours that made it obvious we were on the nightclub strip. We stayed in that section, leaning against the blocks, watching everything and everyone.

Soon after our arrival we heard screaming and yelling. We noticed a girl who seemed very nervous, sitting on the sidewalk with a guy. We ran toward them to see if they were okay. The guy's face was bleeding and the girl had lost a shoe. Two men were watching them from a distance. The guy repeatedly got up from the sidewalk and the girl would pull him down.

"They'll be coming back," said the girl, panicking. "I need my shoe!"

The assailants confirmed what the girl had said: they were going back for them, and they didn't seem too happy. The RLSHs then asked the couple what happened. The guy said they attacked him when he hadn't done anything. The two men approached and Black Dawg intercepted them and asked them what was going on. They said that one of them hit on the girl, not knowing that she wasn't alone, and her boyfriend just attacked them.

Motor Mouth and Black Dawg weren't going to let another fight happen. Motor Mouth spoke to the two men, telling them to leave the couple alone.

The couple was very thankful. The girl asked the superheroes who they were. Motor Mouth explained. She said they were the best superheroes ever and thanked them again and again.

Cheshire Cat and I started to look for her shoe and found it about 20 feet away. When we came back, Cheshire Cat treated the boyfriend with first aid and the superheroes stopped two on-foot police officers to let them sort this out. Since no one wanted to press charges, nothing happened.

Returning to the cement blocks, we waited for a while, observing the people coming and going out of bars, tipsy and drunk, having fun or being sick. I asked Motor Mouth about the California Initiative, the team I was going to visit in a couple of days.

I knew there was conflict between the two groups, but I didn't know exactly why. I found out that NightBug had approached Motor Mouth to patrol with him and the team.

"He very rarely ever came out on patrols," said MM. "After a while, he told me that the reason was because he was doing it all in secret and his wife didn't know anything about it. He would make excuses so that his wife would think he was somewhere else and he went on patrol — maybe two or three times — with us. When the world premiere of the HBO documentary happened in San Diego, he was going to go see it with his wife.

"We didn't patrol with him ever again after that. He told me he was leaving the team. Now, it's only hearsay, but it seems like it had to do with his wife, as she felt that they could do a better job than what I was doing with the Protectorate and that they probably wanted to start something on their own accord."

Motor Mouth was talking normally. He didn't look angry and would sometimes add, "So be it." He also added, "There is more than enough room in the Bay Area for more than one team."

The problem started when they patrolled all together to give food to the homeless — Motor Mouth, the Ray, NightBug, NightBug's wife, Rock N Roll, and one other person — and Motor Mouth said he felt that Rock was too controlling.

"I brought the majority of the handout, but the Ray and I brought the majority of the supplies. I felt like the CAI [California Initiative] wanted to paint me as someone who is not co-operative, that doesn't want to listen. The thing is that I have bent over backwards more than enough for people."

As we were having this conversation, a group of about seven men walked by. Some seemed agitated, some even aggressive. We decided to follow them. Barely two minutes later they stopped in front of the exit of an indoor parking garage, where they met another group of men. Two of them were yelling at each other. Suddenly, one took out a gun, pointing it at his opponent, and then the other pulled out a pistol. I was so close to the gunmen that if I knew anything about guns, I would have been able to tell you what they were carrying. One of the gunmen ran inside, and the other one left the scene. Black Dawg ran after the last one to be able to tell two police officers he approached afterward where the gunman was going. Some girls remained onsite and Motor Mouth asked them questions. We followed the group of people to make sure everything was back to normal and continued patrolling the rest of the night in another area.

When we dropped Black Dawg off later that night, we parked the car and decided to go for a walk in his neighbourhood. It was about 1 a.m. and the streets were completely empty. Motor Mouth and Black Dawg told me stories of the shootings and other violent incidents that had happened at some of the houses we walked by. It felt like I was in an area where even if something happened to you on the street and you screamed for help, nobody would come to your rescue, and people would be too worried for their own lives. It was not a very nice feeling.

We left the area and dropped off Cheshire Cat. Then Motor Mouth and I drove around the city and talked about his life.

As a child, Motor Mouth was considered a geek by his peers because he and his friends loved to play with action figures and read comic books, instead of playing sports. He was also from a bad neighbourhood where kids mostly came from broken homes, sometimes basically living on their own or even getting beaten by their grandparents. Motor Mouth explained: "They had all this frustration built up that they did not have an outlet for, so what would they do? They would go to school and beat the crap out of other kids."

Like many other superheroes, he was also bullied at school, through elementary and most of junior high, until he started to fight back against his assailants. His father taught him how to defend himself and how to throw proper punches. He would also defend his friends who were bullied.

"I would have kids chasing me home, especially when I was in elementary school," he recalled. "I remember when we had portable trailers that were classrooms. On the back lot of the school, this kid would chase me around just to beat me up. One time, he chased me under a portable and I refused to come out from under it for the rest of the day. Another time, a kid had a mathematical compass with the metal spike. He had positioned it in his bag so that it was sticking out from the bottom of his backpack, and he swung it around and partially cut my side open. On another occasion, kids would throw rocks at me and my friends as well. I would personally like to think that we as Real Life Super Heroes are out there to try and be the anti-bullies in the adult world. We are out there trying to make sure that these predatory people do not have a chance to go ahead and pounce on someone and take advantage of them."

Thankfully, Motor Mouth had good role models. His mother and father were both registered nurses, each with decades of experience. He would see them doing good deeds for people, like buying food for a neighbour who couldn't afford it, without asking for anything in return. They participated in Habitat for Humanity as a family, with Motor Mouth helping to build houses.

But when he was 19 years old, two events changed him. He had a friend who floated back and forth between living on the streets and living with her father. She was doing drugs, but had told Motor Mouth that she was cleaning up her act and looking for a job. He spoke to his boss at a fast food place, and the boss agreed to meet with her for an interview. Motor Mouth stopped by her place on his way home. Noticing the front door was partially open, he walked in and saw her lying on a mattress next to her boyfriend, who was stoned and playing video games. He tried talking to the boyfriend, but got no response back, as if he wasn't even there. He went to his friend and started shaking her hand, but it was cold. He saw a bandana with a syringe and realized she used heroin. She had overdosed. She was dead.

On another day, his cousin and two friends were coming back from a corner store. His two nieces had been playing outside and were going back into the house when a car drove by. Two guys hopped out of the car and shot at them. His cousin and two friends ran to protect the little girls and took them inside the house, but his cousin was shot in the back a handful of times. He had been facing the door, trying to prevent the shooters from getting inside the house. The shooters ended up kicking in the door, and the cousin crawled over to a coffee table. The gunmen put their feet on his back and shot him in the back of the head.

Motor Mouth's father had told him about the Guardian Angels, who had been patrolling the streets for over 35 years, wearing their prominent red berets and red coats. They are similar to superheroes but have a more restricted code. That started to get Motor Mouth thinking and eventually led to the idea of becoming a RLSH.

He liked the idea of having a costume. "To me, the person behind the mask doesn't really matter. Motor Mouth is an anonymous face. He could technically be anyone. If I go ahead and I walk around using my real name then that real person has frailties. That real person has faults. Real people have something they are attached to. Whereas Motor Mouth, in my opinion, is everything that is good about myself and more. It's everything that I ever wanted to be and it makes me feel better about myself. It makes me realize that I can help people selflessly and without having to give my name."

And Motor Mouth has a kind of "superpower" that gives him the ability to memorize specific things: he was diagnosed with Asperger's syndrome. Also having insomnia, he often spends his nights on the computer, surfing the Web or reading and learning facts. On top of that, having over 15 years of security experience, practising self-defence and a little bit of boxing and wrestling in the past has helped him achieve his goals. Even skating taught him practical things, such as how to fall without hurting himself. From age 5 to 18, he was a figure skater, nationally ranked four times.

Travelling all over the country between the ages of 17 and 20 gave him a more worldly perspective. "You hear stories about what's happening overseas and you start realizing that things are no different where you go. It doesn't matter if you're in Vancouver, Canada, Mexico City, Brazil, Australia, or San Francisco; there is stuff happening all around the globe. This is one of the reasons why I think people like the Guardian Angels and Real Life Super Heroes are needed worldwide."

We talked about the dangers of the job, and I asked him about how he dealt with the fact that his girlfriend has a four-year-old daughter who lives with them.

MM: I treat her like she is my own. I buy her clothes and I get her dressed in the morning to go to day care. I read her bedtime stories and I sing along with the Muppets with her in the car. And she loves superheroes. We sit and watch all these little animated DC comics movies.

NF: Does she know what you do?

MM: Yes. And when she sees me getting suited up to go out at night, sometimes, she'll say: "Daddy, where are you going?" I'll say: "I'm going out to fight crime." And she'll say: "Ah, because you're a superhero, right?" And I'll say: "Yes, I'm a superhero."

NF: Aren't you afraid she's going to tell people?

MM: Not really. I mean … I've heard her say it to a few people before, but I just laugh it off. Sometimes, she'll be playing with her Green Lantern toy and put on her Green Lantern mask and her little Captain America helmet with her little shield to go with it. I'll play with her and she'll have me put the shield on. So, if she says: "Daddy is a superhero," I say: "Yeah, we play dress-up."

On my last day with Motor Mouth, he took me to meet his parents. His mother is a real pleasure, very nice and welcoming. We sat on the couch in the living room, and Motor Mouth left to give us privacy, but would come back every so often to check up on us. His mother confirmed many things he had told me about his past, such as the fact he had been in the Scouts and then was an Eagle Scout. She showed me the plaque from 1995, when he was the Pacific Coast champion for intermediate junior Olympic ice dancing. He also received a history award at school.

But his mother also told me that he would often leave home for short periods when he was 17 years old. Then Motor Mouth sat with us and surprised me with a story about something that had happened in another city.

"And then I got stupid and tried killing myself. That's when the halfway home found me. I was doped up and my girlfriend's family just dumped me in an alleyway," he recalled.

"It was in December, a few months before his 18th birthday," his mother continued. "The shelter called us and said 'get a one-way ticket, put it in his name, and we will put him on the plane.' They sent him home. He was rebellious and rambunctious. By the time January came around, he didn't go back to high school. He ended up getting his California high school proficiency and his GED. Then he'd taken child development classes and he began working with kids with emotional and mental disabilities."

After talking about the weapons that are legal and illegal in some states, Motor Mouth said, "Go ahead. Tell her about how you guys finance a lot of my activities."

Indeed, his parents do. They also order special masks for him, made in New York City, and other pieces of his gear.

> Motor Mouth's mother (Mom): My husband had one of our local embroiderers do the patches they have for their team and paid for those.
> MM: I have brought those to Thanatos and guys in Southern California and all my teammates here in the Bay Area over the years.
> Mom: Sometimes, I worry about him because he can get really hurt, and there is a lot of liability.
> MM: Remember that time I came back with a concussion, because I wrestled that guy down on Market Street?"

I could tell by the look in her eyes that she definitely remembered. "It's just scary because sometimes you don't know what he's going to encounter," she said.

We had to get going, but we talked about other teams and I told Motor Mouth he should go spend New Year's Eve with PJ. He got excited about the idea but said he didn't have the funds for that. He looked at his mother, and they said they would talk about it.

Back in the car, we talked about what his mother had said and I asked him why he tried to kill himself.

"I was much younger. I was living down in Houston, Texas, and I had gone through a period of my life where I was just kind of burning bridges left and right. I was very narrow-minded in perspective of everything around me, and I started coming to the conclusion that I don't know what's best for me. I had screwed over so many people in my personal life, especially my family that had just done nothing but give and give. It was too much for me to handle emotionally.

"I had also started going through a breakup with my girlfriend at the time. I was living with her, and she broke up with me, and I realized I screwed over all these people to be with her, and then she didn't want to be with me. So, in my head, I thought I had nothing left. I locked myself in the bathroom at home and took all of the household chemicals that were underneath the sink, and I put them into a sippy cup and mixed them up. I just plugged my nose and I drank it down, and I started fading in and out of consciousness. My girlfriend's family didn't want to put up with it anymore, so they put me into the back seat of their car, took my duffel bag with all of my things. They drove to downtown Houston and threw me out of the car into the alleyway and just drove off.

"I was delirious for a few days. I was admitted to a psychiatric hospital for a one-week observation and they realized that I was just stressed out and just needed to relax. They put me on medication for a little bit, but I got taken off at a later date."

Motor Mouth never found out who saved him in the alleyway.

"I just remember walking around and dragging my bag one second. The next thing I remember is waking up in a halfway home. There was a doctor talking to me and he was telling me that I was really lucky that the chemicals I drank didn't burn a hole through my stomach and string me up for a long time.

"Another time, I tried hanging myself, but even though I was a Boy Scout, I couldn't get that knot right. I gave up and I just sat down and cried for a bit. I called a friend of mine and went over to his house. We had a few beers and we talked for a while. He was saying things like, 'You've gone and done so many things. You've been to so many places. You have a lot to live for and you have a good family and people who care about and would back you up no matter what, even if you were doing wrong.' And that's when I turned my life around and realized it's not worth it to kill myself. It's a very selfish thing to do. You are not really thinking about the people that you are going to leave behind.

"I think about the old saying, 'What doesn't kill you makes you stronger,' and the reality is that if you can push through those hard times and find ways to make it work, there's always a way to make it work. If you haven't found it, that just means you have to look harder and sometimes you have to change your environment and sometimes you have to change people who are in your life, whether it be friends or family. Sometimes you have to change your perspective. But there is always a way to get around. Always."

He finished on a note that referenced the world of fictional super-heroes. Motor Mouth recounted a moment from one of his favourite comic books, *Watchmen*, with the ruthless antihero Rorschach. "He is trying to figure out why he does what he does. No one tells you to put on a mask, go march around, to help people, and to arrest criminals. What he ends up talking about is the fact that no one out there tells us we have to. We do it because we are compelled to do it. We do it because there's something inside us that tells us that if we don't do this, then we are not doing enough with our lives, we are not doing enough for our society, we are not doing enough for our world. And although I may not agree with everything that Zero says, he made a comment that we live in very extreme times and to counter those extreme times, we need an extreme solution. Well, we are that extreme solution."

I thanked Motor Mouth, who dropped me off at a restaurant by the water and left.

⚡

It was time for me to meet with the publicized Roy Charles Sovari II, a.k.a. the Ray, who had been a RLSII for only two months. The skinny, young-looking man arrived, and we chose a table on the patio with an amazing view of the water.

I had to start with the Occupy incident that had recently brought him national attention. As the Ray explained it, he spent part of the day stopping people from breaking store windows and attacking each other. Later on, he saw a couple running, who fell on the ground and curled up to protect themselves from other runners. He had seen police officers attacking people in New York City previously, and he noticed police officers advancing aggressively toward the couple.

The Ray (Ray): I know the difference between running at someone and charging at someone. So I immediately ran for the occupiers who had fallen down, and I intervened between the officer and the protesters. I'm not the kind of person to stand there and watch and let that happen. And we usually ask superheroes to try to use verbal or just our presence, but that wasn't going to work that time. So I just skipped the first two steps and went into the physical. I charged the officer and kicked him off the people he was doing his stuff to. I kicked him in the side stomach area, so the ribs, and it wasn't meant to damage him in any way. If I wanted to damage him, I could've kicked him in his head or his leg. After that, I didn't put my shield up in a defensive position, I just stood there with my arms at my side. The officer was a little bit off-balance, but he just stood there and looked at me in awe and we just kind of stood there for a second and then he started taking aggressive action toward me. He was trying to hit my shield and that's all he was doing. The next thing I remember is falling to the ground. I did a roll to get up onto my knees, but then I was hit down again to my face and I was just knocked out.

NF: By whom? The police?

Ray: My lawyer was talking to some other lawyers who said they saw the whole thing and he said that three to five officers came up behind me and just tore me down and started beating me, so that explains why I went down so fast.

People in the RLSH community were, once again, on both sides: those who agreed with the Ray's actions and those who didn't. Those who agreed said that Real Life Super Heroes need to protect those who are attacked by anyone, even if the attacker is a police officer. Many who disagreed did so because the Ray had a piece of armour they felt he shouldn't have had, and because Motor Mouth wasn't with him and the Ray was still a young recruit. I asked him about the racist comment he made during an interview.

Thanatos.
(Photo by Peter Tangen)

Phoenix Jones.
(Photo by Peter Tangen)

A masked Nadia Fezzani on the streets of Seattle.
(Photo by Ryan McNamee)

Nadia Fezzani (centre) during her first patrol with the Rain City Superhero Movement.
(Photo by Ryan McNamee)

Phantom Zero.
(Photo by Peter Tangen)

Nyx.
(Photo by Peter Tangen)

Mr. Xtreme.
(Photo by Peter Tangen)

Geist.
(Photo by Peter Tangen)

The Golden Don.
(Photo by Nadia Fezzani)

Ray: The writer viewed me as a racist because I made comments she misinterpreted. In my area, there are these huge groups of black people who are beating my friends and stealing at gunpoint. And so I guess she viewed me as racist because to some people it might sound unbelievable, but that's what is happening. One time I was talking about a story when about 40 or 60 black people came down our skate park and there was this hill in concrete and it has dead grass so it's really light-coloured, and it was in the middle of summer, and then a mob of black people just came down there. She asked me to describe what it looked like and I told her that there were so many people that they turned day into night. I guess it could have been perceived as racist, but I just tend not to care about those things.

NF: Did you mean it in a racist manner or did it just come out that way?

Ray: I was just trying to describe what it looked like, but of course she didn't use it like that. I think it's ridiculous that you have to be this careful. Amongst my friends, we make fun of each other all the time.

I was a little surprised by his comment. I felt like I had to explain something to him: "But it's different with friends, because you know each other and how much you mean something or if you're joking. When someone doesn't know you at all, they don't know how to read what you are saying."

Sometimes he sounded like a little kid. He was, in fact, young, but of legal age. I learned that he was home-schooled and only hung out with a few people. Depending on the extent of his surroundings, I thought maybe he hadn't had the chance to broaden his horizons or to become comfortable around people different from himself.

The Ray's parents were both in the navy, so he moved around a lot until he was 13 years old, at which time the family moved to a poor neighbourhood. He was bullied constantly in the Scouts, but he wouldn't fight back.

He described the bullying: "Living as a Mormon, I developed certain standards, like I don't drink, I don't smoke, I don't do drugs. And I always do good things for people. I don't hurt anyone. When I was old enough to start Cub Scouts, I kind of did things by myself. I did get bullied, but I wouldn't hurt anyone. I would give them a chance to correct themselves, as I would let them bully me and then I would ask them to stop. When they wouldn't stop, that's when I would have to take action and that's kind of where I developed my ability to defend myself. Also, my dad did martial arts since he was 16 and still continues to do it, so he taught me some stuff on how to defend myself. I was smaller than them."

And he is still short today, at only 5'5".

> Ray: When I started getting out into the world more, by going to the skate park and hanging out with friends, I started to see all of the crazy stuff happening. I have this friend who was at the skate park and he actually got beaten up by a whole bunch of people just because they didn't have anything else better to do. They beat him up, took his iPod, and broke his skateboard.
>
> NF: And do you think that has an impact on what you are doing today?
>
> Ray: Most definitely. Apart from me getting confident to defend myself, I began looking around, and I saw people that were smaller like me and were also being picked on. They couldn't do anything about it because they didn't have the training or the experience. So I started defending others who were getting hurt or put down. That is definitely what encouraged me to want to be a superhero apart from me seeing my friends get beaten up by numerous people.

I remembered Motor Mouth telling me that the Ray's heart was certainly in the right place, but he needed some direction. The thing that had made him decide to really go forward with becoming a RLSH was the day he was in a Safeway and saw people stealing and eating food before just walking out. The police were called but didn't do anything.

He recalled: "I was talking with a cop friend of mine and I was told sometimes they don't care about robberies if the people have money in their pockets. That is categorized as a petty theft and they don't do much for that. That could be one reason why the police didn't do anything about it."

Now, as a RLSH, the Ray feels like he has a bigger sense of purpose, and it makes him feel good, especially when he defends people or helps less fortunate ones. To achieve his goal and defend himself, he made a stun baton. "When attackers see that really long stick just lighting up and big noises and lighting, it definitely scares them off," he said. But the Ray's problem was that he didn't look into the legalities of his new weapon. In California, extendable batons are forbidden, and his was considered an "experimental weapon."

The Ray is a good example of mistakes that can happen when new, inexperienced superheroes work on their own. We finished our interview and I had to get going to patrol with the California Initiative that night.

⚡

Later that night, I arrived at the beautiful home of NightBug and Rock N Roll. They had just finished a big dinner with a few friends and Rock N Roll's adorable children.

The decor was modern and nice, and the place was clean. Rock N Roll works as a massage therapist. She also works sometimes as a bartender, and the couple has a rock band that often does shows. NightBug works in retail customer service.

Once the dinner guests left, Rock N Roll, NightBug, and I got ready to patrol, accompanied by Eon, someone I had never heard of before.

Rock N Roll rejects the RLSH label and prefers instead "X-Alt" for Extreme Altruist. I asked her to explain the distinction to me.

"Most Real Life Super Heroes think the same way," said Rock. "It really doesn't bother me that much, but I think Real Life Super Hero is just something that is easy to recognize. If I go around telling anybody I'm an Extreme Altruist or X-Alt, they will say, 'What the hell are you?' But there are some people who don't like the fact that you have given yourself a superhero title."

It was time to put the gear on. As usual, NightBug put on his red mask made of heat-moulded ABS plastic, formed to his cheeks and nose.

In order to imitate his favourite superhero, Spider-Man, NightBug had his mask fashioned with an insect-like appearance. It was designed and created by Dave Montgomery of the Black Monday Society in Salt Lake City. Multiple eyeholes in the mask simulated the face of a spider. Apart from his matching red pants, NightBug wore all black, including his fingerless gloves.

Rock, on the other hand, didn't mind showing the upper part of her face as well as her long, wavy sandy-blond hair. She hid her lower face with a red-and-black piece of fabric and wore regular clothes to cover her voluptuous 5'5" body. They introduced me to Eon, clad all in black, with padded knees and elbows, and goggles. He was tall and I could tell he was in good shape. Vector, another group member, decided to stay and babysit Rock N Roll's two little children to let the others go out.

I took the opportunity during the drive to ask them questions about how Rock N Roll discovered that NightBug was a Real Life Super Hero.

NightBug started: "I told Rock about the superhero documentary, and the premiere was in San Francisco. A month beforehand, I said, 'There's this movie coming out about superheroes. It sounds kind of interesting.' And she said, 'Okay.' She knows I'm a big geek for that sort of thing. My teammates knew about my plan. We went there and sat down during the movie. I waited until the credits and I excused myself to go to the restroom and then ..."

Rock N Roll took over telling the story. "I was thinking, 'Okay, hurry up!' The director of the documentary, Motor Mouth, and his team were there for a Q&A panel. They lined up on stage, and the audience was really receptive. I wanted to ask them questions. My husband was still away. I was hoping he was okay."

She was looking at a guy on stage, and there was something about him she really liked, including his physique. Five minutes went by. Then ten minutes. She started thinking that her husband was missing something great. Then she saw Motor Mouth and another man hugging, right before Motor Mouth introduced NightBug.

"I raised my hand and I told him that I thought what they were doing was amazing," she said. "I thanked them for that. The Q&A ended. I thought it would be ironic if my husband had gotten hurt by somebody in the lobby while all these superheroes were in the theatre talking. So I got out of there and I heard my husband's voice. I turned around and I heard him talking to the director, but it was that NightBug guy! I have been through a lot and have been shocked, and very little shocks me anymore. I think that was a punch in the stomach that I had never felt in my life. Because I realized that the fact he hugged Motor Mouth meant he is familiar and that they were friends and — oh my God, how long has this been going on for?"

NightBug recalled how funny it was for him that he was standing in front of her the whole time and she didn't recognize him with the mask on.

On their way home after the movie, Rock was silent. NightBug would ask her to say something, but all she could think was: *I feel like he's my best friend and I thought there were no secrets. Once you get that taken away, what else are you capable of keeping from me?*

"I had no cause to even question anything else," she said. "I know everyone keeps certain secrets, but this was a big one. At the same time, it was the coolest thing, and I thought I had to get in on this."

NightBug told her that he would stop doing it if she wanted him to. But instead Rock wanted to take part in it, too. After all, they had been martial arts partners for over 15 years, practising five different fighting styles.

"I'm not foolish though. I know anyone can take a gun to the face," she said. "About 15 years ago, my family and I lost a couple of friends who were murdered, and authorities haven't found the killers yet."

NightBug and Rock brought me to some train tracks where they often patrol. It was a popular place for drug users. The husband and wife team told me that their goal was to safely dispose of the discarded needles that have caused problems in the area. Since they usually worked with more people, tonight was only a patrol to show me the ropes. "We have one person to watch for trains and to watch our back. People can't see what you're doing under the overpass here, so that's why prostitution and everything else is pretty big out here," Rock said as we walked under a viaduct. Rock and NightBug protect themselves with puncture-resistant gloves, pick up the needles, and put them in a sharps container obtained from a local hospital. They then bring them back to the hospital for disposal. They also find other tools that are used by drug users.

⚡

The next day Rock and NightBug drove a minivan and had lots of sandwiches, pastries, and jackets to give away. We drove downtown accompanied by Vector, Seva Sharon, and Thomas Old School and went straight to the area where most of the homeless people hang out. We were unpacking the car when Rock noticed a woman who appeared distraught. She was walking fast and practically dragging her crying daughter along behind her. The little girl didn't have a coat on, and their clothes were quite shabby. Although it wasn't very cold outside, it was still December. Rock stopped the woman and asked her if she'd like a winter coat for her daughter. The woman looked at her, almost tearful, and said yes, because the little one didn't have any outdoor clothing. Rock gave her one, along with a Christmas gift, some food, and dessert. The woman and her little girl left looking very happy. It brought tears to my eyes because it was beautiful, because the girl might not have gotten a coat otherwise, and also because I didn't think anyone should be that poor.

We moved on and gave food to people standing in front of buildings and others hanging out in a very big park. We saw another child who appeared to be without a coat, and Rock had the right size for this little boy. She gave three coats and sandwiches to the adult couple with him. Within an hour, we had given everything we had.

Walking in front of a building, Rock told me about something that had happened about a month earlier. They had seen a father with his two children, about three and seven, in the entrance of a building where the family stayed. They were from an Asian country, coming to the United States when the father was promised a great job. But once he arrived in the country, everything fell apart. They were now living on the street, and one of the children didn't have any shoes. The Initiative bought him a pair of shoes. They came back twice to help them, but the family wasn't there anymore. A journalist had written an article about them in a newspaper, and Rock hoped that someone had reacted to that article and helped them out.

Next we went for lunch at a restaurant, where I interviewed both Rock and NightBug.

"My mom would never let anybody be homeless or hungry. She would take them in, feed them, try to help them get jobs, or help them get on their feet, and we would always have someone staying with us,"

Rock recalled.

Her parents divorced when she was nine years old. Her father refused to pay child support, and as a result Rock N Roll and her mother moved around a lot. But her mother was strong. She was a survivor. Rock's mother was in the Philippines when the Japanese invaded, and she lost a cousin in front of her. She had shrapnel in her arm and a fragment in her back. She had seen babies killed with bayonets. Her grandfather had died at Pearl Harbor, and her grandmother raised her three children alone and made a fortune. She had the best attitude in the world and fought for everybody. All of that made Rock want to fight for people, too.

"It's not like I think I can stop crime everywhere," she said, "but if any woman is going to try, I am more qualified than someone who is smaller, quieter, and not as trained. That's why it just clicked for me."

Like most Real Life Super Heroes, Rock experienced many difficult times as a youngster. When she was five years old and her sister was seven, they had two uncles who forced them to go into the basement. "He was sitting on top of me, trying to undress me and pulled off my underwear, and I still remember the look on his face like he was not in control of himself. Then my little brother came down the stairs to get his train set. My uncle jumped off of me," she remembered. Another uncle tried to kiss her with his tongue. After that, she avoided having contact with them during family events by staying in her room.

Rock was born with a sixth finger she could not move. She also has a first name that kids liked to made fun of. Because of that, she was bullied. In sixth grade, she threatened to cut off the finger herself if her parents wouldn't do anything about it. They had it removed. She went to a tough school where there were metal detectors because of past gun violence long before most American schools started doing so. She started to hang out with her sister, who was strong and tough, and who showed Rock how to not let anyone hurt her.

Rock's first husband, the father of her two oldest children, was a great husband for their first three years together until he began drinking. His addiction turned him into an abusive partner. First it was verbal abuse, and then it escalated. Rock left him after the first time he laid hands on her.

"He got drunk and went crazy," she recalled. "He tried to choke me to death. The neighbour knocked on the door and interrupted it. He snapped out of it and realized what he was doing. So he bolted and ran out the door. The neighbour took me to the emergency room. She is a nurse and she saw that I had a black eye and marks on my neck. My mom did not raise her daughters to be beaten by men or to have anyone put their hands on them. So that was it. I was done with him."

She then started studying martial arts.

I asked her if she had any advice to give to someone who might find themselves in a similar situation.

"Find somewhere to talk about it first, because there is so much you blame yourself for. That's how the abuser makes you feel — like it was your fault. If it makes you feel stronger and more powerful, get some kind of training where you can protect yourself. But you have to work on your mind first so that no one can make you feel like that again. So that's the advice I would give: get help!"

NightBug had a different kind of upbringing. Unlike many of the RLSHs I'd been meeting, Night's youth was at least relatively idyllic: stable and secure. His route into the community of superheroes was through comic books. He was a fan of Spider-Man in particular and he liked the idea of fighting for others. "It just seems like the right thing to do," he said.

NightBug heard about the phenomenon of RLSHs and looked to see if any were active near him. The superhero he met first was none other than Motor Mouth.

Although NightBug had a solid family environment, they lived in a bit of a rough area. Their home's garage had been broken into at least three times. The thieves stole tools from Night's father and used them to break into other homes in the area. His car was also burglarized. Some of the tough kids in the area were prone to sporadic violence, too.

"I would get sucker-punched as the rough kids walked around looking for someone who's not paying attention. Then they fled the scene. But I was never seriously beat up."

NightBug seemed at a loss for words. I gave him time to think as it felt like something was on the tip of his tongue.

Rock and I exchanged a knowing look, so I turned back to her.

NF: I feel like Rock has something to say.

Rock N Roll (RNR): I want to ask him something. I was so excited, as I thought maybe there was going to be something I was going to learn.

NF: I can see that he's measuring everything he says.

RNR: I have a group of friends who are therapists, and when we had a rough spot, we went to this therapist friend of mine and she kept telling him, "You close up a lot to everybody, including her. You don't open up." It was the same thing with his brother I've known for twenty-something years.

NightBug (NB): It's not just me. My family has a history of sweeping things.

So he talked more about thieves he had encountered, like one who went into his parents' backyard. The little NightBug had seen him through the window and his father had gone to see what was happening.

We continued talking about the RLSH community and eventually came to the topic of Real Life Super Villains. NightBug explained that not every supervillain is useful. Some just pump up their own egos and need attention while others are there to make a difference.

"Some of them are clearly there to call people out when they need to be called out," said NightBug. "That is important. Like the Eye of Doom. I actually like them more than other people. I like that they bring things to our attention that aren't necessarily obvious, issues that need to be talked about. They call people out when they need to and they give props to people who deserve it.

"The Eye has called BS on some people who have lied. It happens so often, to be honest. There is always a new group of RLSHs that jump in and don't realize that it's dangerous and that it requires work. You need to pay a little bit more attention and be a little bit more skilled than that to keep doing what you're doing. And the villains are good at identifying them."

"I can't wait to meet with them," added Rock. "They are behind the scenes and they do so much good. And they are so entertaining! Their videos make me laugh. Their radio show is hilarious and a half an hour is not enough!"

I remained wary about the idea of meeting with a self-described villain. But maybe it would be okay.... And maybe my experience with supervillains would change my life.

8

XTREME JUSTICE LEAGUE

I remember feeling a bit sorry for Mr. Xtreme because of the way the HBO documentary about RLSHs portrayed him. His way of speaking made him come across as a nervous fast-talker. They made a point of showing his terribly messy apartment and then called attention to the fact that he had to leave his home to move back in with his mother. It was easy to imagine people laughing in their living rooms at Mr. Xtreme's efforts.

I wasn't quite sure what to expect when I went to San Diego to meet with him. Had the documentary really miscast him as a loveable loser? I was sure of one thing: he seemed to be about as genuine a person as I'd come across in this community, and a man with an enormous heart. He seemed like the kind of guy who would give the shirt off his back to a complete stranger.

Mr. Xtreme picked me up at the bus station in San Diego. While Mr. Xtreme may carry a few extra pounds, his regular martial arts training still gave him a formidable frame. He seemed quite strong, and he exuded a genuine demeanour. I had told him he didn't have to come and get me because the hotel was quite far from the bus terminal, but he had insisted. "That's what superheroes have to do! Help in any way they can, and not just fight violence," he said. I could tell he was nervous around me. At least that part of his portrayal in the film was true.

Mr. Xtreme took his name from the defunct Xtreme Football League (XFL) and Mr. Fantastic from the Fantastic Four comics. He calls his group the Xtreme Justice League in reference to the Justice League of the DC Comics world. Mr. Xtreme has made a lot of sacrifices to do what he does. So naturally, I asked him why.

> Mr. Xtreme (X): I feel like it's the right thing to do in a world where there's a lot of apathy, indifference, and a lot of violent victimization of innocent people. I take this very personally, as I have been a victim of violence myself. I have grown up in a household of abuse and bullied at school, and I was the person who just didn't fit in. I'm willing to double down, and I put my life on the line on more than one occasion before.
>
> NF: It can get violent sometimes. Did anything violent happen recently?
>
> X: Urban Avenger and I we were breaking up a domestic violence situation. This guy was being very violent, and he was trying to fight people on the street, too. We tried to talk him down. I told him the police were coming and that it wasn't worth going to jail. He was just giving me the F word and telling me to get out of the way. He started attacking me and Urban Avenger by fist, aggressive shoving, pushing. And then he came up and started throwing a flurry of punches. So I shoved him and head-butted him with my helmet. The guy attacked me. I pushed him back. He grabbed Urban Avenger and was punching him. Urban pulled a stun gun and then, out of nowhere, someone from the crowd came up and clocked this guy in the head.
>
> The first guy calmed down pretty fast because the pepper spray was starting to sink in and we had to help the guy and give him first aid because of the pepper spray

and the hit in the head. Another time, a guy pulled a knife on us. We put our lives on the line, but luckily none of us have been seriously injured. The person who has gotten the worst of it is Urban Avenger. He has been hit on the head a number of times, and he has had his ribs bruised, but nothing serious. He's a pretty tough guy and he's very committed.

I admired their dedication and their desire to help others. But when he started talking about knives, I imagined all the things that could go horribly wrong. Death and injury were possibilities, but what if a RLSH found themselves facing assault charges? I asked Mr. Xtreme about that. Would he be willing to be arrested and even incarcerated in the course of doing his self-appointed duties?

He responded: "I am willing to do what is right. If I have to end up getting arrested to protect somebody's life, then yes. If I had to intervene on an officer that is going too far, yes, I would do that. But I would make sure that we handle it smartly and not just on a whim. If there was a cop taking it too far and getting pretty violent, we would also have to take into consideration that he is armed and that we are dealing with a situation where force is going to be used. We want to make sure that we have all of our bases covered."

When I asked Mr. Xtreme if he considered himself a vigilante, he answered that they are not judges or executioners — what most people consider a vigilante to be — and they would use reasonable force or legal weapons to defend people within the law. "We don't violate people's rights. We try to be as professional as we can be. We consider ourselves almost like peacemakers. Crime fighters, yes, but similar to the Guardian Angels in a way, but we wear costumes and carry less-than-lethal weapons."

Since he said he was willing to potentially interfere with a police officer, I had to ask. "How is your relationship with the police?" He said it had improved, that the authorities were starting to warm up to him, and that they had collaborated in the past. "No police department can endorse us or any community watch groups that take a proactive stance against violent crime and do physical intervention. It is just too much of a liability.

If one of us made a mistake, that's going to make the police look bad and cause them problems."

Similar to Thanatos, Mr. Xtreme has never been convicted, but he has been arrested while on duty. The Xtreme Justice League was conducting a training exercise behind a mall. Someone spotted them and thought that a robbery was in progress. The police briefly detained the group until they could verify what was happening.

I spent a few hours alone in my room that night, until Mr. Xtreme picked me up for our first patrol. I already had my bulletproof vest on under my coat, but I didn't wear my mask or anything else that would make me stand out in a crowd. We parked on the street in a quiet downtown area and put our equipment on outside the car. He had a cobra stunlight, a blinding flashlight that was equipped with both a red laser to scare or disorient opponents and a pepper-spray canister. He put on his black chin protector and added ski goggles that were covered by a picture of huge fake eyes. The rest of his get up was patterned off of military-style fatigues. He wore a green cape to accompany it, with green plastic greaves to protect his legs, black leather-spiked gauntlet bracers and a black bulletproof vest. Two long green rectangles were featured on the front of his vest: one said "Xtreme Justice League" and the other said "Evil Suppression Unit." Pictures of two victims accompanied the rectangles.

One of the victims he honours is Kitty Genovese, whose case has become synonymous with bystander apathy.

Mr. Xtreme described Genovese's situation: "She was getting off of work really late. She left her car and was going back home when some guy followed her, stabbed her, and raped her. This attack was going on for about 30 minutes. She screamed for help and a bunch of people heard it and didn't do anything."

Indeed, at least a dozen people may have heard her. But most thought it was a small domestic fight or just a group of friends leaving the bar. One man saw the initial stabbing and screamed at the attacker, who left right away. But the attacker came back to repeatedly stab and sexually assault Genovese. Another man saw the rape. Both witnesses called the police, but no one went out to try to help her. Today we call it Genovese Syndrome, when bystanders see what's happening, but don't do anything to save the victim's life.

"There are many Kitty Genoveses out there," said Mr. Xtreme. "This happened in Richmond, California, just a year or two years ago. There was a 15-year-old student, she was gang raped by a bunch of guys and nobody did anything. In fact, people were so low that they were filming it, taking pictures, and texting each other about it. It's ridiculous that that type of apathy even exists. I see a lot of that. It seems like people don't care about their fellow human beings. At work, a security guard got locked inside of an electrical room and called the maintenance guy to get him out. He didn't even go. He felt like this was an inconvenience to him, so he just left him in there. It's not the same as what happened to Kitty Genovese, but it's the concept. What if this guy had a heart attack? People can help and they choose not to."

You could tell by his eyes that Mr. Xtreme was both angry and disappointed in the apathy he fights against. He was sad — sad for the state of the world he lives in. He relayed another sad tale: "14-year-old Amber Dubois was the victim of a murderer and rapist who also killed and raped Chelsea King, who was 17. Both were found in the San Diego County. He had also molested a 13-year-old."

Mr. Xtreme and another RLSH participated in the search for Amber Dubois and printed many flyers to try to find her.

"The list is very extensive," he went on. "Seven-year-old Danielle van Dam, nine-year-old Jessica Lunsford, seven-year-old Megan Kanka, nine-year-old Amber Hagerman. And so many others."

One of the girls he mentioned, Megan Kanka, was the victim who inspired Megan's Law, identifying sexual predators to people in the United States. Amber Alerts (America's Missing: Broadcast Emergency Response), a child abduction alert system, are eponymous of Amber Hagerman.

"How do you remember all those names?" I asked.

"I can't forget that, because of the circumstances that surrounded their violent deaths. It's part of what keeps me personally motivated to keep fighting crime, keep patrolling, and keep running campaigns. What if it was my daughter, my cousin, my niece, or whoever was close to me?"

Mr. Xtreme understands suffering and pain. As a child, he would escape through comic books, such as Spider-Man, X-Men, Batman, and G.I. Joe. Later on he got more into the Power Rangers and Ninja Turtles, and then darker comics like Nightwing, Wild Dog, and Mirage Man. But reality

wasn't so easy. He has been victimized numerous times with assaults, robbery, molestation, and even a hit-and-run.

"I can understand the feeling of the loss of sense of security," he said.

As an Asian child, he didn't fit in. At one point he was the only Asian
in his school. He was constantly bullied. A bully took his lunch money
and lunch box. He would beat him up, spit in his face, and ridicule him
because the little Mr. Xtreme was overweight and of a different ethnicity.
Mr. Xtreme grew up as a loner.

"I felt like shit," he said. "I still do. I felt like no one understood me. I
felt unloved, I had low self-esteem and I felt made fun of. In elementary
school, a kid was beating me up and pushing me around, so I went up
and I stabbed him with a pencil. He went down crying and in pain. He
stopped bothering me."

"It's sad that you had to go through violence to stop violence." I
observed.

"It is. Then I would get home and my mother was always away for work.
My father was working a lot, too. He was burnt out and exhausted, and he
took it out on me and my brother. He abused us mentally and physically.
He used to beat the crap out of me. He talked down to me. When I was in
junior high, we got into a pretty violent fight together. I remember when
my brother and I were playing around and ended up breaking a pane of
glass. My father got home and he was pissed. He beat the crap out of my
brother. Then he took me to the bathroom and started beating me down,
punching me, hitting me. Another time, I came home from school and
my room was a mess. He started yelling and screaming. He beat me with
a belt. One day, my brother and I were just joking around with my dad
and I said, 'Hey, I think someone put a booger in your food,' and he spit
it out and started hitting me."

Eventually, he and his father patched things up. But the weight of the
abuse and bullying he experienced has cast a long shadow on Mr. Xtreme's
life, including on his romantic life.

He continued. "I felt like I was just an accident and people did not
understand me. I was suicidal, many years ago."

"Have you ever tried to end your life?" I asked.

"Other than patrolling in bad neighbourhoods by myself?" he said
sarcastically. "At one point, I was taking more risks out there, on patrol.

I was trying to break up fights by myself and I would run to chase down cars."

Mr. Xtreme was also molested at seven years old by his male babysitter, which made him struggle with his sexuality.

"I just bottled it up and tried to keep it to myself. Today, being a leader of people and groups like XJL, I have run into a lot of people who have been down on their luck. People look at us for leadership, for role models, for a way to give back. It's somewhat a self-therapy. I have had my share of personal problems, but instead of resorting to drugs, alcohol, and a criminal lifestyle, I went for something positive."

As if that weren't enough, he was also the victim of a violent crime. The Bloods (a.k.a. the Reds) jumped Mr. Xtreme when he was 17 years old and beat him up. They threatened him with a knife and told him to take his blue shirt off — the colour of their enemies. The young Mr. Xtreme was traumatized. He was also held at gunpoint by street thugs wearing ski masks for his car and his cellphone.

But what I found out is that, after all this, Mr. Xtreme joined the Guardian Angels in 1998. He has seen a lot with them, from violent assaults to a rape in progress.

"We were on patrol and some passerby came up to us and said he had heard a scream over by the alley. My partner, who was also a trained nurse, and I went through the dark alley. We heard that woman scream. We got closer and I just saw her lying down on her side while the guy was stomping on her head. I yelled, 'Hey!' and the guy started running. I chased him. He was running pretty fast. My partner was helping the victim with medical aid. Then three or more members of my group joined into the chase and we ended up getting the aggressor against a wall. The police had already been called and they arrested him."

Demonstrating a great deal of trust, he showed me a thank-you letter addressed to his team (with their real names), as well as a newspaper clip about that event, which he carefully kept between protective plastic sheets.

He got involved with the Guardian Angels in Los Angeles, having admired them since he was eight years old.

"I heard about them being in my hometown of San Diego, California, and about their efforts to organize a group in Tijuana, Mexico. I just became fascinated with the idea and the concept of citizens patrolling the streets, protecting the neighbourhoods, being a positive role model, without weapons. The Guardian Angels gave me the training, the knowledge, and the experience I needed. They also trained me in Jeet Kune Do, a freestyle martial art founded by Bruce Lee, in Wing Chun, a martial art often used in movies, in Brazilian jiu jitsu, and in street fighting."

After being with the Guardian Angels for three years, Mr. Xtreme opened a chapter in San Diego in 2001. In 2006 he was promoted to California Regional Director. He patrolled in many cities, such as Chicago, New York, Las Vegas, and Phoenix. He was selected to train a group in South Africa, where he spent a month. He also went to London to work with the Guardian Angels.

"We've gotten into quite a few situations where we have made a positive impact," he said.

But what surprised me most was that he is still part of the Guardian Angels *and* leading the Xtreme Justice League.

"The RLSHs … do they know that you are doing work for the Guardian Angels?"

"No," he said.

Of course, both groups are fighting for the same cause. But taking care of one group was already a lot of work. I couldn't imagine taking care of two groups. I guess it explains why he's always busy.

"The groups are different, but there are a lot of similarities, from my experience, and I look at it from the eyes of a Guardian Angel *and* from the eyes of Mr. Xtreme. We deal with the same things out there on patrol, the same drama and the same difficulties with running a group of volunteers and trying to manage them."

⚡

Mr. Xtreme received a call and I heard him say, "We're on our way!" After walking a couple of blocks, I noticed the silhouette of two people, standing in front of the Hall of Justice. Grim, a physically imposing man standing 6'2" and weighing around 220 pounds, was standing there dressed in black and blue with silver reflective stripes. His mask resembled the upper half of a skull. He had a flashlight and a very small video camera screwed to the top of his helmet. His lower face was hidden with black fabric cut into strips, as though it had been through a paper shredder. The other man, Rouroni, was about 5'9", with a slim build. He was wearing all black as well, but wore an Asian conical hat. I could not see his face; it was hidden behind a black piece of fabric and only his eyes were visible.

I had the chance to chat with Rouroni while we were walking the streets. He seemed so young, though he tried to appear very serious. He never smiled. Grim was vigilant on patrol while Mr. Xtreme took the time to explain more about the team and their tasks.

We patrolled the nightclub district and were on hand when the clubs closed. The night was incident-free, other than the occasional drunk woman trying to steal Mr. Xtreme's goggles.

> NF: Ugh … I would have no patience for that.
>
> X: And that is just part of it. We take a lot of verbal abuse, with people saying bad things to us, laughing at us, and thinking that we are nuts. They call us every name. We just ignore it and brush it off and just soldier on. We don't have time to get emotional about dumb things like that. And in a way, I think it's good that people notice us; we dress like this so we can be highly visible, so they know what we are doing
>
> NF: Mr. Xtreme, what is your biggest fear?
>
> X: Nothing shocks me anymore because I'm starting to get detached. That is my biggest fear — getting emotionally detached and not caring anymore.
>
> NF: If that ever happens, will you stop defending people?
>
> X: No. I would just keep reverting back to thinking in detail about the victims, about what they went through, the trauma that they live. Think about what if it happened to me, to my family, the close ones, and thinking about how I would feel if I was victimized. That is going to keep me from not caring. There is a quote I really like, by Edwin Torres from the New York State

Supreme Court: "A society that loses its sense of outrage is doomed to extinction."

Some girls in a truck passed by and screamed out loud: "I love you, superheroes! Make my dreams come true!" Some pedestrians asked to take a picture with them. Others would ask them what they represent.

NF: I heard that you were invited to speak at City Hall.
X: Yes. The deputy mayor of Chula Vista, Rudy Ramirez, invited us. He saw us patrolling during a groper campaign to find a sex offender. One of his interns was giving a presentation about sex offenders, so they wanted our input about what we are doing to keep people safe. We definitely felt that we had a big sense of accomplishment there, as a team. Very few RLSHs have been invited by the local government to speak.
NF: And you offer rewards?
X: We have offered $1,000 to $1,500 to people who can give us information to arrest sexual offenders.
NF: Does that come straight out of your pockets?
X: Yes. But now I think I'll be saving up, because I have $24 in my bank account. Actually, maybe I can put that up for reward also....

He was sarcastic about his lack of funds. Unfortunately, as of yet, no one has come forward with useful information in the case of the local groper.

X: A man was targeting Asian women and doing home invasion and robberies. We ran a campaign for that. A few TV stations picked it up.
NF: And how do you justify to yourself spending that money when you don't have any?
X: I just feel like it needs to get done. I'm not just going to sit around and wait for somebody to give me that donation. We have to find a way to make things

work. So that is how I justify it. I'm going to do the best I can to make sure that I at least have the money to support myself to cover my basic expenses. Whatever I can muster up, I can use toward what I need for the cause.

Mr. Xtreme said he was also part of some activist groups before, such as Amnesty International. He found it too political, and his tasks were mostly to write letters when he wanted something more active, like stopping fights, robberies, or sexual assaults.

The patrol was done for the night. Nothing happened, which is a good thing. We all walked back to the Hall of Justice, said goodbye, and walked toward the cars.

⚡

The next day, Mr. Xtreme picked me up after he was finished work and brought me to a location where I immediately felt uncomfortable. Although it was a bright, sunny day, the area was absolutely rundown. The few scattered buildings were in bad shape, and everything was dilapidated. There were many, many empty lots. Most of the cars that passed were as rundown as the buildings and looked ready to fall apart.

"This is South East San Diego," said Mr. Xtreme. "There are quite a few gangs in this area and lots of crime. Someone has been murdered on each corner of that street. It's known as the 'Four Corners of Death.' We're just going to take a quick walk and kind of get a feel of the area. Right now, we are on a scout patrol, to gather information about a future patrol area."

We walked around to see the lay of the land and Mr. Xtreme pointed out that I should never come here alone. We definitely agreed on that. Then we drove to Lincoln Park, on Willie James Jones Avenue.

"Willie James Jones was a valedictorian at Lincoln Park High School, many years ago," explained my guide. "The day after his graduation, he was gunned down by gang members when leaving a school function in the evening. I think they mistook him for a rival gang member. The city named the street after him. Lincoln Park is definitely a very high crime area in

San Diego. A lot of people have been killed in this community because of gang violence."

Next we went to Costco to buy water bottles and snacks to distribute to the homeless. Mr. Xtreme had previously told me that being a RLSH was a full-time job for him. I could tell it was. When he's not at work, he spends his time recruiting new members, training people, and generally investigating areas of the city where members of the public might need his help. What little time is left to him, he spends just across the Mexican border, where his girlfriend lives.

One of his future goals is to establish an after-school club for local youth. His idea is to help prevent vulnerable kids from being recruited into criminal gangs. "I was watching this special about MS-13," he said, "probably the most violent vicious street gang in America. They were going to high schools, trying to recruit kids as young as 12 years old and sometimes even younger than that. They were trying to lure them into some party and tell them about the glories of joining a gang: alcohol, money, sex, power, guns, and glorifying violence.

"I heard that they often ended up holding them against their will, and they get some girl and the boys end up raping the girl. Then they become a member of MS-13 and the gang crews give them what they are missing at home. These children come from dysfunctional families. The gang recruiters say they can fill that void, the gap of love they've been missing. We have to come up with some type of a program to intercept the gang recruiters because the recruits are the future generations of bad guys, street mutants, drug dealers, murderers, rapists, and so forth."

The Xtreme Justice League wants to give those children a sense of purpose and a positive, safe space outside the reach of the local gangs. They want to show them that doing good, doing positive, and being a hero is cool and rewarding.

> NF: Would you say that most Real Life Super Heroes come from dysfunctional families?
> X: Definitely, I would say. Quite a few people that I have met in the movement come from dysfunctional homes and families. They seek the RLSH community

and the teams that are involved. It is almost a circuit family. That said, we don't deny that some of the people that have worked with us have criminal backgrounds. We're not ashamed of that at all. We actually encourage people to go out and try to give back to society and try to straighten out their lives and do something positive. The Xtreme Justice League will not disqualify you just for the mere fact that you have a criminal record; it depends on what it is. There are certain people that we won't accept: rapists, sex offenders, and murderers. Other than that, as long as they are not on parole, probation, or have warrants, if they've already done their time and now they are just trying to straighten out their lives and give back, we will give them a chance. They have to pass the interview, be willing to be a team player, work hard, and have a good attitude. They have to prove themselves to us every day.

NF: Earlier, you told me some tasks were boring. What are they?

X: Going to Costco and picking up a couple of cases of water to get ready for the handout. We're going to the bank now so I can have the money to be able to print off some recruiting flyers. Getting on the computer and sifting through dozens of crime articles and statuses. Sitting down and making the schedule to tell the guys what we are going to do this week.

In the car Mr. Xtreme explained that the newbies are first on a probationary period where they hang around. Recruits go on patrol with the team to see what is needed in their training. The team evaluates the new ones while they earn the team's trust. The recruits have to show that they are dedicated and that they can work under pressure. They have to put in a minimum of one night per week consistently over a period of three to six months, depending on their progress.

X: To be able to graduate, they have to show that they're taking a true and genuine interest in what they're doing, that they are not just here to show off and that they are respectful. For instance, Grim was taking initiative to post ads on Craigslist and get flyers made. He looked for crime reports and stats, and would suggest things that can benefit and contribute to the growth of Xtreme Justice. If you show that type of initiative, that definitely gives you points. I know the training is tough. We train hard and we do scenario training. Some have bumps on the head and bruised or cracked ribs. The intensity can vary: little to no intensity, moderate, or rough. Grim has been with us for about six months. He graduated in two months and we gave him his Xtreme Justice League patch. Then we moved him up into a higher position of leadership. He is now our patrol sergeant. He is also on our back XJL leadership committee, which means he's a core member and a leader who has voting rights.

NF: Do you have examples of when you had to kick someone off the team?

X: We've had to do so when somebody was using excessive force during interventions. We've had to kick somebody out for just being a flake, like not being committed and not showing up. There were guys that were just lying and BSing and telling stories and then trying to create problems and trying to do something like bum money. People that we have had to talk to over and over again and people who have been disrespectful, and not just one time.

I noticed that Mr. Xtreme wasn't talking fast anymore. He didn't seem to be as nervous around me. He was much more laid back. I knew he'd had a bad experience with a journalist in the past.

"Today," he continued, "the main focus is scenario training in preparation for our New Year's Eve patrol. It's not meant to get you in shape, to build up strength and endurance or to make you look ripped. For that, I encourage people to exercise on their own, join a gym, work out. Together, we have to do more tactical training."

We drove around to see another area. Most of the buildings had bars in their windows — even the church.

"We're in the area where a shooting occurred in 2009. From what I understood, there was a house party and the victim got into a fight with another girl. When she walked outside, someone drove up and opened fire and drove off. A couple stabbings also happened in this area. Both of them were on December 23 and December 24. One was with a young man around 20 years old who was walking down the street. It was in this community, in the Mountain View area. Some guys in an SUV saw him, they yelled at him, threw something at him, got out, stabbed him, robbed him, and drove off."

The Mountain View Area. I found it an odd coincidence that it had the same name as the cemetery where I had met Thanatos.

"The other situation was during another house party," continued Mr. Xtreme. "I heard a hundred youth were attending this house party. Members crashed it, a fight broke out and three people got stabbed."

I noticed even the fire station had bars on the windows.

"Vandalism is very common in San Diego," said Mr. Xtreme.

⚡

Later on the team assembled in a large public park. Surprisingly, Rouroni still had his mask on; he was the only one hiding his face. He didn't wear his hat, however, so I could see his short light-brown hair. He seemed a little shy. The four of us were ready to participate in the training. I had told them to treat me like one of their own, but I could tell they were going easier on me. The guys showed me how to defend myself in many different ways, depending on the size of the attacker. At first, we were practising on a body opponent bag. Then, the young men pretended to be attackers and I had to show them that I was able to control the situation. If I failed to defend myself, I had to do it all over again. And again. And again. Until I succeeded a few times in a row. For example, I had to be able to get an attacker to the ground while he attempted to strangle me. I also had to practise falling to the ground to simulate the response to an active shooting. We trained for a couple of hours. I was impressed by what they'd taught me, and I definitely felt sore and bruised the next day.

⚡

Grim and I went for a coffee so I could interview him. The small café we chose was quiet and had few patrons, so it offered enough privacy.

Grim explained the origins of his nickname. Apparently he was upset about something and made a sound like "grrrrm." Someone heard him, and since they didn't know his name, they called him "the Grrrrm guy." Just like other RLSHs, Grim is motivated by doing the right thing. "It was just the way I was raised," he said.

His father was a sheriff and his mother was a police officer. One of his uncles was a homicide detective. Grim may have followed in their footsteps had he not chosen instead to enlist in the navy where he spent six years as a nuclear plant operator in a submarine. Now being a super-hero allows him to help others, but without the constraints of being a police officer. He doesn't have a boss, and he doesn't have to do things he doesn't agree with.

But his life could have turned another way. Living in a "redneck area," as he called it, where he and his family were the only black people in a predominantly white, Mexican, and aboriginal neighbourhood, he was beaten up, jumped on, or harassed every day. But when he would tell his parents he got into a fight, they would tell him, "Well, stop getting into fights!" until they understood, many years later, that he was actually being bullied.

In the meantime, he became confused and isolated. He was angry at times, but never enough to really feel hate. When he was able to, he would run away from his attackers. "If you don't make it easy for them, they won't want to do it anymore."

During his youth, bullies had thrown him down a hill, hit him with rocks and baseball bats, and burnt his arm with a lit cigarette. "It sucks," he said.

Beyond bullying, he also got held up twice at gunpoint. When he was 16, he was held up in the bathroom of a McDonald's. A man was waiting in ambush behind the bathroom door. When Grim entered, he was robbed. He had a mere $5 in his wallet at the time.

The experiences have made Grim a cautious man. He started wearing his father's bulletproof vest around all the time. But although he thinks some of these things might have contributed to what he does today, he likes to think that he would patrol even if nothing had ever happened to him.

The incident that really changed his life occurred soon after he started hanging out with serious drug dealers. "I don't know what I was looking for, but I liked hanging out with them," he said. "No one screwed them over." He would go to their houses all the time, smoke pot, drink alcohol, and play video games.

Shortly after high school, he was hanging out at a restaurant with one of his buddies. "I will call him D, like the Devil," he told me. "He's a horrible human being, always treating people like crap, I don't really know why I was friends with him. I guess I just thought he was cool. We were eating with a guy I didn't really know. Some guy in a truck parked outside came in and gave D a bad look. D started yelling all types of crazy stuff and was looking at him in a threatening way. He didn't shut up and kept on belittling that guy who then walked out."

When Grim asked his friend what was up with that guy, he said "fuck him" and that he was nothing. A few minutes later, two guys returned to the truck and got out with guns.

"They just started shooting straight into the restaurant. We jumped behind the tables and then D started to shoot back. I was in over my head, wondering what I was going to do. I didn't know who these guys were ... I could be going to jail ... all these thoughts were going through my mind. D slid me a gun and we both shot right at them. One of us hit one of them in the shoulder. It was almost instant. He went down and I went down at the same time. The other guy pulled him back into the truck and drove off."

Grim was lucky. That was one of those days when he was wearing one of his dad's bulletproof vests. He told his mother about it, and she told him never to tell his father. "I don't know what he thinks happened to the vest, but it's gone!" the superhero said.

"I felt like someone drove a car onto my chest and parked it there. It felt like I was getting crushed in the chest for a long time. It was burning.

The bullet stopped in the vest and I could see the bullet. It was sitting there. I still have the scar from it. That freaked me out. I didn't know who the other guy was, but as soon as someone found out, one — or both of us — would have gone to jail. I had to get out of there."

That was when he joined the navy. Today he patrols and is writing a book on the manifestation of good, evil, and in between. It's about mental powers and the ability to read minds and control thoughts, all based on metaphysics and subatomic physics.

⚡

It was time for us to meet up with the rest of the guys again. I was somewhat excited since this was going to be my first weekend patrol with them, and weekends were usually when things happened. Also, I was finally going to meet Urban Avenger, someone I had communicated with and heard about from others many times during my research.

Mr. Xtreme had told me that Urban Avenger was one of the most dedicated RLSHs that he had ever met or worked with. Urban had a reputation as a tirelessly devoted superhero. He rarely missed opportunities to patrol, either with Mr. Xtreme or on his own. He patrols when he's sick and when he's injured, and he has invested a lot of time and energy in the team. Mr. Xtreme said he has shown a lot of courage and that he is almost fearless. He spoke of him glowingly.

Urban and the rest of the team met in front of the Hall of Justice. He was a little shorter than I had imagined at only 5'7", but he could move quickly. All in red and black, he was hard to miss. He had special goggles that gave the impression of being fluorescent under the light. His black mask and red hood protected his identity. He also wore a red motocross chest protector.

We introduced ourselves formally while we were walking toward the club district. On our way we came across a drunk man in his sixties who could barely stand on his own. The superheroes asked him if he was okay and whether he wanted to call someone to get him. The man didn't want any help. They sat him down on a bench at a bus stop so he'd have some shelter and be more comfortable as he sobered up. Two men approached us as we were walking and politely asked us what we were up to. Mr. Xtreme took the time to explain it to them and gave them a business card in case they eventually wanted to join.

We were on 5th Avenue, where a lot of problems happen on the weekends. Mr. Xtreme showed me the places where incidents had occurred in the past and told me stories about them.

Later the team intervened in a fight outside of a restaurant. Two men were arguing when one of them punched the other in the face. The superheroes separated the men. The puncher's hand was bleeding, so Grim took out his medical kit and bandaged up the cut. Soon the police arrived and they seemed to appreciate the witness statements from the team. The stories the two men told were contradictory and less than helpful. The police officers were very courteous toward the RLSHs and never asked them to remove their masks. One of the officers said, "Your team is getting bigger!"

We walked for a while after that and nothing happened. The long night was turning cold, and we all needed a water break. We went to the store to get something to drink, and Urban Avenger and I took the opportunity to go into the lobby of a big hotel, grab a table in an empty area, and do an interview.

He started by telling me that he had met Mr. Xtreme and many other RLSHs in 2010 at the Comic-Con in San Diego. His first patrol took place that same night.

"It was almost spiritual," he said, "I would help people here and there in my life, but it felt so good to be part of something bigger than myself. I had been to church and that was fine, but after a while it did not really seem like my kind of thing. This fills some kind of void in my life."

Urban Avenger's childhood, just like the other superheroes, was not typical. His parents divorced when he was two years old, so he never experienced the usual family life. He was raised by his mother and grandmother. His father was occasionally around but was not the greatest example. He was sometimes abusive, especially toward Urban's brother.

"One time, when I was five or six, I was acting up and he hit me with a belt until he left big bruises on my butt. But that was really the worst it ever got. I never really thought he was a bad father, but he was not always there. I lived in Los Angeles for most of my younger life until I was about nine and then we moved to Texas for about a year and moved here for the last 18 years. I was born here and I consider myself a native San Diegan. I was in LA for seven years and I try not to think about it because I hate Los Angeles."

Los Angeles reminds him of the LA Riots and the Rodney King beating, among other things. "What sticks in my mind are the ambulances flying by my house every single day, the riots being on the news, and the gangs that my family had to deal with, which was part of the reason why we left, since gangs tried to attack us at our house. So maybe deep down, this is me getting back at it. I don't want to see people victimized like my family was all those years."

Urban Avenger suddenly looked serious and reflective. "Maybe my life plays much more influence on my superhero life then I thought. My father was shot by police officers." He explained that his father had re-married a few years before he died. Despite being an alcoholic, he was able to stop drinking for a few years before his wedding. But his new wife drank a lot. Urban's father had sustained a serious hand injury, which prevented him from following his dream of being an auto mechanic. He became depressed.

"I guess the night that he died he had gotten really, really drunk and really depressed. He was having an argument with his wife, and he owned a shotgun. He pulled it out and was threatening to kill himself, so she called the police. From what I understand, the police made their way into the house, did not announce themselves, saw the guy and just opened fire. They shot him nine times, and he died."

Urban was 18 years old at the time.

His relationship with his mother was better, and she has always been in the picture. Although they were very close, their relationship became a little more complicated when his mother became vocally critical of his father. "I did not want to hate my dad. So I think that kind of made a little wedge between us," he said.

But the family trouble wasn't done there. His older brother had been friends with a couple of people who were involved with gangs. When Urban was about eight years old, the gang members came to their house, yelling. "They had a knife and they broke my grandmother's arm," he recalled.

Living in that world, as a kid, he used to dress up with a cape, a towel, a bandana, and a mask. He would go to his neighbours' houses and say, "I'm a superhero!" The neighbours told him, "No, you're not. Stop messing around!" And then the little Urban Avenger thought, "Awww. Damn. My secret identity is spoiled."

He started reading comics when he was about seven.

"I started reading simple stuff like Disney comics, like Scrooge McDuck, Darkwing Duck. Darkwing and the Ninja Turtles were a huge influence on me, because they were for kids. I then watched X-Men, Spider-Man, and Batman. I always loved superheroes and comic books. I started growing out of comic books when I was about 19 or 20, but I still loved superheroes. When I was in high school I drew myself as a superhero, as what I wanted to be. It was a little bit different than what I had to become, because that character used guns and had no problem killing people."

Surprised, I asked, "Why?"

"I was probably acting out teenage aggression. I got in trouble a few times at school for drawing guns and swords, especially since that was around the time of Columbine. That event had a big impact on my school life." During the Columbine High School massacre in Colorado in 1999, two high school boys killed 12 students and one teacher, and injured 24 others before committing suicide.

Urban Avenger was in school at the time, watching the shooting unfold live on TV. Although he, like the Columbine shooters, was bullied, Urban realized that he would never seek that kind of revenge on his tormentors. Still, he became curious about the psychology of the two boys who'd wreaked so much havoc in Colorado.

"You'd see the interviews from the survivors. People were threatened, and they saw all of these people dying in front of them. But their mindset did not change. The shooters were picked on and bullied. The students did not learn anything from that incident. For example, there was one football player that was on one of the two shooters' hit lists. After everyone had died and it was all over, that person still called them names. He would call them 'faggots' or something like that. So somebody came at you with a gun, and now that they are dead and your friends are dead, you are still not changing who you are. Bullying drove them to do that. What the hell is wrong with you? I did not want history to repeat itself, especially with myself or any of my friends."

Like many young people, Urban and some of his friends began wearing trench coats like the ones worn by the Columbine shooters. "We thought it was rebellious," he said. "We were already the kind of people who stood out and everyone knew who we were, but we did not know who any of them were. We were popular without really trying to be, but not in a good way. People thought of us as social outcasts and nerds and geeks, and I was not a normal kid in any way ever in my life. I was never normal. I was very introverted, and it wasn't until after high school that I started becoming more extroverted and expressing myself and being comfortable with who I am."

He spent most of his time playing video games and drawing. He was also into theatre. Urban Avenger, like so many RLSHs, was bullied quite severely. One of the bullies lived in the same apartment complex as Urban's family. The bully beat him up and generally terrorized Urban and his family. He'd cause disturbances at their apartment window and even vandalized the family car repeatedly.

We talked more about the bully.

> Urban Avenger (UA): I actually ran into him when I was working, a few years after graduation. I heard that he went to prison for hijacking a semitrailer. He had been imprisoned for a few years, which really did not surprise me, and he had not changed in 10 years. He was the exact same person he always was, and that was the last time I've seen him, six or seven years ago.
>
> Bullying is still one of those things that get to me. Even now, when it's like 14 years later. Today, if I see someone being harassed or picked on, I will do something about it, whether it's just giving an opinion or to interfere or even physically stop them. Bullying is not going to happen when I'm around, regardless of who it is.
>
> NF: Some people question why you do this and put yourself in danger.

UA: I'm not worried about myself getting killed. I wear armour, I've got training, I've got back up, I got teammates who are there for me and never steered me wrong. I can't live with myself knowing that if I don't go out every night, who knows who would be seriously hurt or going to the hospital, because I didn't happen to be there at that moment.

NF: But you know you can't always be out patrolling or be everywhere!

UA: There are times where I'd taken a night off and somebody got hurt a few blocks away from where I was, and I felt so guilty for not being there. I know I can't be out all the time, but at the same time, why couldn't I be there? I have to live with that. I don't want to see anybody get hurt, I don't want to see anybody going to the hospital. It sucks. That's really what drives me.

His superhero idea came to him after seeing the movie *Kick-Ass*, where people with no superpowers decide to become crime fighters.

"I was saying, 'Hey, why not? I could totally do that! That would be so awesome!' I felt like a little kid again. My friend asked me, 'Haven't you heard of Mr. Xtreme?' and then he explained to me what he was doing. I checked online and found the Real Life Super Heroes. I was completely blown away! I got in touch with Mr. Xtreme, I felt like such a geek!"

The movie *Kick-Ass* also taught him how *not* to be a superhero. "The first day *Kick-Ass* went out, he was stabbed and hit by a car. He didn't know what he was doing," said Urban Avenger.

Since then, Urban Avenger has learned American boxing and jiu jitsu.

Before becoming a Real Life Super Hero, he admitted he had defended himself the extreme way over 10 years ago.

UA: I did defend myself in an overly violent manner once, which resulted in somebody going to the hospital. I learned a lot of self-control after that. I stabbed a guy. It was self-defence. He came at me and pushed me. I pulled a knife on him. It was in somebody else's house, and I didn't want to hurt anyone or to be hurt. So I decided to walk away. Then he kicked me in the back and sent me flying down some steps. We fought and I stabbed him. I didn't even realize it until I saw the knife in my hand and the blood. The guy went to the hospital.

NF: And what about you?

UA: I went to jail for 50 days. The judge said these were very special circumstances in a self-defence and I had used excessive force, but at the same time he realized that this guy had come at me a couple of times and I was trying to protect my brother.

Since then, he said he was able to have his felony expunged from his records. However, he still has to pay restitution for the other guy's medical bills to the tune of $33,000.

"That whole period of my life taught me to control my anger. I was very hotheaded and ill-tempered back then. Mostly, it was anger. For a long time, I could not even touch a knife, let alone carry one. I didn't want to accidentally stab somebody, so I was very paranoid. After a couple of years, I got comfortable with carrying one. I now carry one on my belt full-time."

He feels he is now able to control his anger. It takes a lot to set him off or get him mad. In fact, as a superhero, he said he has never been angry.

When I asked him why he didn't want to become a police officer, he had many reasons: not being on patrol and pushing a pencil, being assigned only to a specific area, not being in control of his schedule, policies, procedures, paperwork, etc.

While we were on the subject of policies and politics, I brought up the topic of the Real Life Super Villains to see what he thought about them.

"When I first got involved, I thought they all sucked. I was saying, 'Guys, leave that guy alone!' Then I realized they were doing a service to the community. They're weeding out a lot of the fakes and people who really need to be exposed because, let's face it, there are a lot of bullshitters in the community. And the supervillains do a very good job of pointing those out."

⚡

We were preparing to shut down the patrol for the night. It was almost 4:30 a.m. On our way back to our cars, Rouroni noticed a dog throwing up on a restaurant patio. The poor animal looked so pitiful and malnourished, but it was clearly a friendly animal. He wagged his tail excitedly as we approached.

We could see staff milling around inside the closed restaurant, so the guys knocked and asked if anyone knew the dog. They said he'd been out there most of the day, but that nobody knew whom he belonged to. We gave the animal water, which he gratefully lapped up, and we found some food for him, too. We waited for what seemed to be forever, in case the owner came back, and eventually we decided to call the animal shelter.

Mr. Xtreme told us that it could take a few hours before shelter staff could come. We didn't want to leave the dog alone. A short time later a couple approached and were moved by the dog's situation. The woman, tearing up, said she couldn't leave the dog there, though they already had a dog. They talked with us for a few minutes, explained that they had a house and a large yard for the dog to play in, as well as other animals to play with. They wanted to take him in because in a lot of shelters dogs die or are euthanized or, worse, they end up in the hands of people who want to do them harm. We then had to say *adios* to this beautiful dog, but we were pleased with the outcome.

It was December 30. Originally, I was supposed to patrol with this group for New Year's Eve, but I found out that Motor Mouth really wanted to patrol with Phoenix Jones. Since I was the one who had put the idea in his head, I wanted to be there, too. I decided to leave for Seattle the next day. When we were all back at the Hall of Justice, I finally remembered the Justice League in comic books had also met in front of the Hall of Justice. Just before leaving, I received a pleasant surprise: my Xtreme Justice League badge! It was a professional-looking black leather pocket that holds IDs inside, with the team logo on the outside, and a chain to wear it around my neck. Mr. Xtreme invited me to join them any time.

Who knew that some of the training I had learned would come in handy sooner than I imagined....

9

PHOENIX JONES — PART II

Coming back from San Diego, I was running late for New Year's Eve at Phoenix Jones's home. I did not want to miss the midnight countdown and be stuck celebrating the new year with the cab driver. Fortunately, I made it on time. PJ's crew was all there: the boys, their girlfriends or wives, and Motor Mouth. I was glad he had decided to join us.

The women each had a few beers, but the men weren't drinking anything, since they were going out on patrol. I was in the dining room, absentmindedly snacking away when suddenly the guys broke into song.

"Sometimes I wish I could ... Turn back time ..."

This was the second time I'd heard PJ sing, so I rushed to the living room to enjoy the free show! I sat down on the couch and watched the men dancing beside each other, as if they had practised their choreography ahead of time. I couldn't believe my eyes! Those tough guys, singing and dancing in line, to a Backstreet Boys song!

PJ invited Motor Mouth to join in. He was the only one standing against the wall in the living room, not wanting to move. "No way!" he said. I could have already told them that there was no way that tough Motor Mouth would participate in such a spectacle.

Before long, we were counting down to the new year. "3-2-1 ... HAPPY NEW YEAR!" We were holding confetti poppers and enjoying the dawn of a new year. After everybody exchanged their best wishes, we were ready for the patrol.

Tonight was going to be special. We were anticipating a busy night since New Year's Eve often brings the potential for trouble. PJ wanted the women to walk one block ahead of the men so that people wouldn't know we were all together. He also didn't want the women to do anything but walk and enjoy their night. The women could not be officially on patrol since they had been drinking. The men didn't drink, and, in fact, PJ simply doesn't drink alcohol.

PJ was really excited to hit the streets with a new piece of equipment. He had recently purchased a Baker Batshield. Although it's not a reference to Batman, it does look like a bat. It folds out to provide maximum protection, and they are used by law enforcement.

PJ had asked me to walk ahead with the other women. The streets were relatively busy, but nothing unusual was going on. People were having fun, smiling, laughing, and seemingly having a good time. But I felt like something had changed for me even in the short time I had spent among Real Life Super Heroes. I wasn't normally so watchful and observant while walking around. I am not usually alert to potential crime around me. Maybe I was turning into a bit of a Real Life Super Hero myself! I looked back and noticed the guys interacting with some people. Despite PJ asking me to stick with the other women, I had a job to do, too. So I went back to join PJ and the team.

Everything seemed normal as we were all walking, a little dispersed on the sidewalk, when suddenly, *Bang! Bang! Bang!* The sound of gunshots rang out over the din of the crowd. I didn't know where exactly the sound was coming from, but I knew it was close by. I threw myself to the sidewalk and crawled behind a car. There were about 15 people outside of a bar. Some followed my lead and dove to the ground. I made eye contact with a man hunkering down behind the car next to my hiding place. I could see the fear in his eyes. My heart was racing; my breathing was fast. There were women screaming and running, afraid for their lives. People bolted into alleyways or into any cover they could find. Others simply just ran as far and as fast as possible.

"Get down! Get down!" yelled Phoenix Jones to the crowd. But I was already down. Thoughts whizzed through my head. Where was the shooter?

I had to know where the shooter was. I carefully peered out from my cover until I could see the shooter. Even though he was partially hidden from me behind a fire truck, it was still too risky to make a move. Just because I was wearing a bulletproof vest didn't mean I couldn't take a shot to the head. I also remembered what happened a couple weeks ago when we faced down another gunman. I didn't think Phoenix Jones would be too happy if I took an unnecessary risk while on one of his patrols.

I raised my head, just enough to peek through the bottom of the car's window, but the shooter was still hidden by that fire truck. Everywhere I looked I could see young women scattering in front of the nearby nightclub, running as fast as they could with their high heels and short skirts. I also noticed that the men, in their sneakers, easily outpaced them. Say what you will about Real Life Super Heroes, but I can't imagine any of them taking off and leaving terrified women in their wake!

I still had no idea who the shooter was targeting. Was it us? Was it someone else? What is a random act? There wasn't much I was aware of, right then. I couldn't tell you if it was cold, warm, or windy. I didn't even notice the type of car I was hiding behind. I could have been walking on broken glass and I wouldn't have noticed. In the heat of that moment, I was just looking out for myself.

I could still hear though. I heard gunshots coming from a few feet away. I could feel my breath coming in heavy gusts. My heart was pumping so hard it felt like it would burst out of my chest. When I think back, I don't think the physiological changes came from fear. It was more like an adrenalin rush. A keen awareness of the danger I was in caused a surge of excitement, a strong sense of drive to get out of there alive.

Ryan was filming the scene. The gunshots had slackened and seemed to be farther away. Motor Mouth then decided to go check out the situation. He approached the parked fire truck and looked behind it. The other superheroes and I soon joined him. Thankfully, no one seemed to be injured. Phoenix Jones asked some bystanders where the shooter had gone. He gathered his crew and ran off in the direction the eyewitnesses had pointed. The other women and I stayed at the crime scene. As the police arrived, they closed off the area with yellow police tape, and although we were standing at the corner of the street, all we could see were police officers and their flashing lights hiding the entrance of the alley. While some authorities secured the area, others went to chase the gunman around a building. The Real Life Super Heroes were also running toward the shooter, but they went around the other way to try to cut him off from the other direction. The police caught the shooter.

Time tends to stand still during adrenalin-fuelled moments like this one. Although the incident seemed to last an eternity, the whole thing was over in no more than a few minutes. Oddly enough, during my entire life, only once was I taught what to do in case of a shooting. Two days prior, the Xtreme Justice League in San Diego made me take part in their training, and I was grateful now. It seemed like fortunate timing, and I appreciated their willingness to provide me with practical training.

It was, by far, the craziest New Year's Eve I'd ever had. I thought again about what drives these superheroes to act with so little regard for their own safety. While everyone else fled or took cover, these eccentric guys, with their peculiar outfits, were ready, willing, and able to go to extremes to prevent others from becoming victims of crime.

⚡

On January 1, we took it easy. It had been quite a crazy night and we were all tired. PJ, Purple, and I decided to go out for dinner to one of their favourite places. It was a nice restaurant, with secluded booths enclosed by tall wooden walls.

Even though we had just spent many days patrolling together, I still hadn't really had a chance to sit down and interview the super-couple. We placed our orders, and then I took out my mini-recorder and started an interview that began on January first and ended on January second. We talked into the early hours.

Phoenix wanted us to start the interview with Purple Reign, a name that was chosen in honour of domestic abuse awareness; Purple being the colour used in most domestic violence campaigns, and Reign since Purple is a survivor and now reigns over her life.

The business accountant started talking about her childhood. She recalled her upbringing in a small town in Montana. She came from a big family with old-fashioned and conservative religious values. She revealed that her musician father was an absent figure regardless of whether he was physically present or not. An alcoholic and a drug abuser, he died in a car crash when Purple was only eight years old. Her mother, who had already left him, was struggling to raise the entire family on her own, but she was a good caretaker. All of that made Purple who she is today: solid and understanding. She didn't complain, and she respected her mother for doing so much. When her mother remarried, she had the chance to find a new father figure, someone who took her under his wing.

"I did everything with him," Purple recalled with a dreamy smile on her face. "We worked on cars, we played guys' sports, we rode motorcycles together." Her stepfather had a stabilizing impact on her, even if his presence made her wistful about having missed out on that kind of relationship with her biological father. Purple then flourished. She became an excellent student, studying college-level material as a high school student. It's no wonder she's considered the brains of PJ's operation.

It was events in her early adulthood that motivated her to become a Real Life Super Hero after she'd met Phoenix Jones. Until then Purple hadn't gone public with her story of surviving abuse. It's a hard topic for many survivors, but she'd come to the conclusion that going public with her story was important. She wanted to come forward in order to help other men and women who might be survivors or who might currently find themselves in an abusive situation. Purple was ready to step up.

In most cases, there is a specific reason someone decides to dedicate their life to a cause. In Purple's case, it was a relationship — a bad relationship that became violent. But it wasn't the first time she had been drawn to abusive partners. It was one particularly toxic relationship that eventually pushed Purple to turn her life around. Like so many abusers, Purple's ex-boyfriend was a victim of abuse throughout his childhood. He never got help dealing with the lasting effects of his traumatic upbringing. He was a powder keg of anger and would explode when alcohol entered the mix. "I was such a weak person and he had so much control over me," she recounted. "From being so put down all the time, I became depressed and I had low self-esteem. I got buried from being put down so much."

Like many victims of abuse, Purple's days were filled with name-calling. Her ex-boyfriend used to say things like, "You're no good and if you leave me, nobody will ever want you." He regularly insulted her friends and family members. Purple became isolated from her friends, and often wasn't allowed to go out by herself. On one of the rare nights when she was able to go out with her friends, she was supposed to be home by 10 p.m. As the night went on and she was enjoying herself, she began feeling guilty about staying out. She called him to invite him to join her, but she was with friends who didn't like him, so he refused. He was mad. When she got home around 2 a.m., she was afraid and expected him to be drunk, angry, yelling, and throwing and breaking things.

She finally gathered the courage to go inside. He was lying down on the couch and appeared to be asleep. Afraid, she went to the bedroom and locked the door. He got up, followed her and began knocking on the door. She asked him to leave her alone. He started to yell, "Let me in! Let me in!" When she told him she was scared of him and that she was going to call the police if he didn't stop, he lost what little self-control he had. It was the beginning of a fight that turned her life around.

Purple's boyfriend broke down the door, smashing it to pieces. He blocked the doorframe with his large body and refused to let Purple leave the room. She managed to scramble into the hallway, but he grabbed her phone and broke it. Then he grabbed her and banged her head against the floor while choking her. He told her, "You're not going anywhere." She couldn't breathe and was losing consciousness. Purple recalled reaching a point of physical and mental exhaustion. She could no longer resist and she became passive. Almost like an animal caught by a predator. She resigned herself to whatever fate her cruel partner had in mind for her that night.

The attack continued until she promised not to call the police. When he finally got off of her, Purple ran to the door of her condo, screaming and calling for help, but nobody came to her rescue. "The doors were so thin. I know people heard me. I think that's part of why I try to raise awareness."

The next day, she went to work with a black eye, a bloody nose, and bloody lips. When her co-workers asked her what had happened, like so many living with domestic abuse, she lied. "I said I had been in a car accident," she recalled. "The really sad and embarrassing part was that this happened for a couple of weeks."

Her friends were telling her to leave him. She would leave and then return, after listening to him apologize constantly, saying he would never do it again. "I will get counselling," he would say, "I'll go to anger management."

Like most victims of domestic abuse, she stayed with him because she was afraid. "I thought he was going to track me down and kill me," she said. "I thought if I stayed with him and pretended to be happy, I'd tell him that I forgave him and I'd apologize for what happened — even though now I know none of it was my fault — he'd be happy, and he'd never do anything to hurt me again. I remember thinking 'I will be really unhappy for the rest of my life, but I will be alive, my kid will be okay, and he won't be hurting anybody.' Like I could be the sacrifice to keep him in line from hurting people."

As I listened to Purple's story, I could tell by her facial expression and her voice that she was still hurt about that part of her past, but I could also see how relieved she was to finally break her silence.

Eventually, Purple met with a therapist through her job. The therapist helped her see that what was happening to her was not part of a normal relationship.

"It took a lot of convincing just to build up the courage to stand up against my ex-boyfriend. The day in court, when I had to get the final restraining order, I did not expect him to come, since the room was full of women only, with their advocates. My ex showed up and lied to the judge. He told all of these awful stories, trying to make me sound bad in court. He owed me lots of money. There were thousands and thousands of dollars in damage to my condo because he also broke the bedroom door, the door to my closet, and left holes in the walls. It was all part of the same assault, and I had to pay for all of it. The judge ordered him to pay me back, but he never did. And I'm not going to go after him for it, but it was just one of those situations where I saw him sitting in that court room and it brought back all of that fear. In the end, I got the restraining order and I've never heard from him since."

To this day Purple is hard on herself about her victimization but she's trying to use her voice to give hope to others in similar situations. "Victims have to have hope," Purple said. "In my situation, I didn't have any hope and I didn't think there was a way out. But there is *always* a way out. Losing our sense of worth, not having the confidence or the courage and feeling broken down is the worst place we can be, and I think that we should always know that there is a chance.

"When we handle it in the appropriate manner, like going to the police and filing the right paperwork, documenting what happened, and then having that support around you, there is still a risk, but I think the risk is worse when you stay in that relationship. In my case, I honestly think he would have killed me if I'd stayed with him. At some point, he would have lost it. That risk is not worth it. The risk is worse to stay."

Purple revealed to me that as a minor she was the victim of sexual assault and molestation, and held hostage on two occasions. In those instances she also screamed for help, and no one came to help her. The experiences left her feeling isolated, with no one to turn to.

Abusers often seek out signs of weakness and isolation in their victims. Like Purple's ex-boyfriend, they often make it difficult or impossible for their victims to maintain independent social networks. For that reason, one of the unique parts of Purple's campaign is teaching people to be assertive. She encourages people not to be afraid of intervening because doing something could save lives.

Since she made it public that she has been a victim of abuse, Purple gets dozens of emails daily from women who experience abuse. Purple explained, "They don't know where to go or what to do, so I give them resources in their local community. I've helped a couple women get out of their situations, get into shelters, and get counselling." She counsels them, one-on-one, by email and in person. She raises awareness, as well as money for charity organizations that help people in this situation. "So many people are affected by it," she said. "I had no idea how bad it was. I had no idea of how serious of an issue it was."

She tells people: "Say no! When I was young, being in a religious family, we were taught that you need to respect your elders and do what adults tell you. We were also taught not to let people touch inappropriately, and to say no, but I was not very assertive. I was always afraid of getting in trouble, so when something bad happened to me — and it happened a couple of times — I was too afraid to ask for help. In my situation and with my sister too, if either of us had the courage to speak up then we wouldn't have experienced what we did. So, to young people especially, have the power to say no and speak up!

"I think, as women, we have that women's intuition where we pick up on things right away. In a lot of my situations, especially the one with the really violent boyfriend, I knew in the very beginning that he was bad news. When we first met, he lied about who he was and almost cyber-harassed me for a while. He made these fake girls' profiles to contact me and get me to fall in love with him, saying, 'Aw, he is such a good guy! He's had all of this bad luck.' I started feeling sorry for him, so despite my initial feeling that something was wrong, the passionate side of me took over, and we eventually started dating. First instincts are almost always right, so follow them! I think we can tell if someone is good or bad when we first meet them."

While she was recalling her traumatic past, PJ added occasional remarks about men who abuse women or children. He said no woman should ever have to go through such a thing. Purple looked at me and told me that it breaks PJ's heart every time he hears the story. But then, she told me about the sunshine that came into her life about six months after leaving violence behind.

Phoenix won her heart … after bidding on her at a charity auction event. She was there as her real self, not as Purple Reign.

"For a charity event, along with other women, I donated a date with me for auction. This guy I had never met spent almost $400 on my charity. We went on a first date and the rest is history," remembered Purple.

But what Purple didn't know was that her date was the Real Life Super Hero Phoenix Jones, and he had just been stabbed!

PJ: Surprisingly enough, the stabbing didn't even faze her. [laughs]

Purple Reign (PR): It didn't faze me at all.
PJ: That was a surprise to me. I was in shock about that because I was in a lot of pain. I gave her a piggyback the entire time, and she had no idea that I was bleeding internally.
PR: I was thinking he was so strong.
PJ: I was thinking, "I hope I don't run out of blood before I get home."

We all laughed. But seriously, going on a date after being stabbed? PJ was so excited about his date that he super-glued the skin to prevent further bleeding.

PJ: When I first met Purple, I was living on the roof of a building in Belltown. I had to get up before 6 a.m. to make sure I did not have to pay for parking. Also, my licence was suspended. I would park in Belltown and go out at night and fight crime until my heart was content. I would sleep on the roof in my super-suit. I had to pick up my son in the morning and drive to work. I'd eat food downtown and then go back to fighting crime in the evening and sleeping on top of the building. I volunteered at a soup kitchen on Sundays, part of that is because I didn't want to stay on the roof on Sundays.
NF: Wait … what? [That was one thing I had never heard of before. PJ had lived on a roof, apparently homeless?]
PJ: I did not have a police scanner, I did not know how to find crime, I did not like living where my mother was, I did not like my house because my ex-girlfriend was not very nice, and I just thought I would be close to the action that way.
NF: How long did you do that for?
PJ: Probably four months. That is a long time.

PJ told me he had showered at work. Back then, he wouldn't tell anyone where he was living or what he was doing.

PJ: It was not fun. I got to watch a lot of movies through other people's windows. You know, movies are kind of interesting when you self-narrate them. You think I'm kidding? I am dead serious. I lived on a roof, watching movies through binoculars and self-narrating movies and TV shows that I had never seen before. It was pretty awkward, but that was a different time.

PR: I did not know where he was living when we first met. I just assumed that he lived at his mom's house, and I was a bit confused, but I did not ask for all the details. I thought he was a grown man and I did not want to embarrass him. He would come over and he would watch movies, and we would just lie down and he loved it. Later, he admitted that he would pretend to fall asleep out there. That way I could not kick him out. He did not want to sleep on the rooftop.

As PJ explained it, he was not really homeless. He was paying for an apartment and many other things for his ex-girlfriend and the son they had together, but he preferred to be on top of a building than with his ex-girlfriend.

I asked him how he'd been stabbed before his first date with Purple.

"At the end of the month," PJ said, "the grocery stores get rid of all their baked goods, so I went there and I convinced them to give them to me to give to the homeless. So I have this crazy homeless handout. I was handing out this food and these guys started fighting over it. Then I go down to the gospel mission and hand out the rest of food because I had so much food, it was crazy."

It was a little funny to hear about PJ feeding the homeless at that moment, with his suit on. I remembered hearing about an incident earlier in his career as a superhero where PJ threw food at a homeless man, and publicly said that giving food to the homeless was no super-hero work. He was highly criticized for this, and eventually his attitude toward this aspect of RLSH work changed. He continued telling me about the incident that might have forced him to miss his first date with Purple.

"Two guys were fighting over food, and one pulled out a knife over a piece of bread, when he already had a ton of other food that I'd given him. I ran in there and I was like, 'What are you doing? Break it up!' The guy punched me in the back so I turned around and looked at him, and he had a knife in his hand but he just ran away. So I went to the other guy and said I was going to call the cops, and we were going to get him arrested because he was hiding behind a pillar down the street. It was really weird. The police showed up and arrested him. It was that easy. The cop said he had a knife with blood on it and I said, 'That's weird ...' The cop looked at me and goes, 'You know that you're bleeding?'"

PJ had been punched in the back and slashed, with a really long cut in the lower stomach area, as he turned around. But because of his secret identity, he refused medical help, stayed with the homeless people and brushed it off as if nothing had happened.

"When the cops left, I walked to my car and it started getting to me. I had this moment where I was thinking, 'Okay ... either call the ambulance or you got to man up!' So I went and I found — this was a bad idea, by the way. Don't do this. This is a stupid thing to do — I went into a parking lot, I knew that gravel and mud stops leaking. It irritates the skin and inflames it, but it closes the wound. It is just disgusting. Then I ran to my car and I came home. I was with my ex at that time. I lay down and she sprayed my wound with super glue and we tried stitching it, which was bad. It did not work. It was just really painful, and then we tried to glue it and that didn't work because it was fully open. Then my ex-girlfriend told me I should go to the hospital, as nobody knew my identity. I don't know why I didn't think of it earlier. We just went to the hospital, and they took care of it. I had been really dumb. I told him I had backed into something at my house and I got cut."

I wanted to know more about how the super-couple had met. But the conversation took a turn, and PJ told me about all the times he'd been stabbed or cut while patrolling. I had only heard of one of his stabbing incidents, so I asked him to recount a few of the others.

"Some of them never got publicized," continued PJ, "and I never talk about it because there's no win, and it's not heroic to get stabbed and let the criminal go because you're going to bleed to death. The next time I got stabbed was more publicized; I got stabbed when I was breaking up a fight and there were tons of witnesses. I got stabbed again on another night of patrol after that. My scars are really hard to see because I heal very well."

I asked PJ if I could see a few scars. He didn't mind, so he lifted his shirt. There were a few I could see very clearly. He could tell me the story behind each of them.

> PR: These injuries happened when he was out by himself. After a couple times of coming home with blood, we got a team and he hasn't been seriously injured since.
> PJ: It helps to have teammates around to deflect criminals. When I was flying solo, I could stop one guy. But there could also be eight guys. So then you would never come out of it untouched. Most of my injuries come from multiple attackers. [Looking at Purple] Like the other day when I got punched in the face when you were on patrol with me.
> PR: It's looking better already. [Looking at me] Somebody else just punched him in the face when he was running by. It happens all the time.

Both of them told me about other times that PJ was attacked. But Purple is not worried anymore since he no longer patrols on his own. PJ admitted that if he had kept on doing what he was doing, he would have been dead already. I found it interesting that PJ had been on such a self-destructive path before Purple came into his life. All of the RLSHs I'd met seemed like they were harbouring a lot of past pain.

PJ remembered the first time he took his shirt off in front of Purple.

> PJ: She just stopped and looked at me. Because I would not go to the hospital, I had one that had become infected, and it was leaking this disgusting stuff, and I got tetanus from sleeping on the metal roof. My forearms were lumpy and swollen from all the blocking of weapons because I didn't have any arm guards. I didn't have any money, so I didn't have anything other than a general

bodysuit. My body would've either quit, or I would've died or gotten killed.

PR: At about that same time we were first dating, he also had a concussion.

PJ: I had a serious concussion. I was throwing up, I was sick, and then the next night I was back sleeping on the roof and fighting crime in my super-suit on the streets with the criminals.

PR: I told him we had to go to the hospital because of the tetanus. We had to go and get the right antibiotics. The doctor told him he had to stop.

PJ: The doctor said I was bleeding. I had a subdural hematoma — I was bleeding under the skin. I was suffering from exhaustion and tetanus and I had 7 percent body fat, something really, really, low. Ha, people think I'm in shape now? When we started dating, I was 160 pounds. I am now 205.

But PJ just kept on going. He didn't believe this could actually be happening. But after a doctor friend of Purple's explained to PJ how the body worked and that he was going to shut down, he decided to change his plan of action. He let Purple take care of him and he took nights off.

He used to say he was patrolling five nights a week.

"It was really seven days a week but I didn't want to say it or make it seem like I didn't have a life so I would say, 'Oh yeah, five nights a week or so,' but it was every night. Now I say five nights a week and it's really more like three to five every week."

"On our first date, the date was over at 11 p.m. because he had to fight crime!" said Purple. Looking at PJ, she added, "You were addicted to fighting crime."

And PJ agreed. "Yeah. I was like a crime fighter out of control."

⚡

Purple and PJ each have a child from a previous relationship. Purple accompanies PJ on patrol when the children are with their other parents.

She ends up joining PJ's patrols about half of the time. When not actively patrolling, Purple does research into the latest crime statistics in order to help the team focus on problem areas. "It's really rewarding," she said. "I feel like it really helps the team be successful. Before, when they went on their crime patrols, they kind of went around the city jumping out of bushes and stumbling across the crime. When I got involved, I had access to all these awesome tools and resources. I can see all of the police reports, all of the crime stats. I can put it on a map and see what time of day crimes were happening and how long it takes for the authorities to respond, what happens when they respond, if anyone is arrested, what kind of weapons are involved, if there are any victims, etc. Then I cross-reference that with the weather, with the bus routes, and we've really got it narrowed down where action is. There are different police stations around the city, and those officers have their beats that they have to walk and patrol, and we've got it narrowed down to where we have seen the most violent assaults — muggings, rapes, etc. We chose violent crime because those are what we want to interject in."

By now I'd heard PJ talk at length about what he does. But I was still not clear on why he did it. I wanted PJ to start from the beginning, so I asked him about his childhood.

From birth until the age of five, Ben, the little boy who would become PJ, lived in an orphanage. At some point the people working there found out that his family lived just down the street. "They told me my family couldn't just abandon me like that," said PJ, "so they made me go live with my family."

Curiously enough, Ben had two brothers and two sisters, but he was the only one sent to the orphanage. Soon after returning to live with his birth family, his mother was arrested and convicted of drug charges. She had been selling drugs, using a baby carriage as cover. Two years later Ben's father brought him to a convenience store and left him in the car.

"I heard gunshots," recalled PJ. "I waited in the car. I waited and waited. Finally, the police showed up and asked me, 'What are you doing sitting in the car?' I was like, 'Well … my dad is in the store.' They asked if they could talk to me and I went back to the orphanage — which was cool with me, because I didn't want to live with my family anyway.

"If you're going to rob a store," PJ added, "do not do it in Texas. It's the gun capital of the world. It just goes to show you how the guy [his father] was an idiot.

"My dad taught me a lot of skills that are just generally inappropriate. One of the things he taught us was how to open car doors and then tell certain people, 'Hey, for 10 bucks, I will tell you where the car is; the door is already open.'

"When having that kind of bad influence, you have to make a choice. You can say, 'I'm going to be a product of my environment and grow into a criminal and just be like everyone else,' or you can say, 'No, I'm not going to do that.' I just basically said I'm not going to do that, and because I understand the attraction of crime, I understand the satisfaction you get from crime. I think my dad was very happy with his work. He wasn't in any way trying to reform as a criminal and he died robbing $75 worth of stuff at a convenience store. It's just a stupid thing to do."

Ben was ostracized by the other children in the orphanage. He felt they resented him there because he knew who his parents were. The adults, according to PJ, weren't much better than the children. "It was just a really terrible place," he added, without wanting to give more details.

Ben didn't have many friends. But the boy he hung out with was nicer to Ben than he was to anyone else in the bunch. "It's kind of crazy because he was the most psychotic," remembered PJ. "I thought he would probably turn out to be a serial killer," he said.

"I used to be more emotional than I am now. My friend enjoyed hurting animals when they made noise. If they were silent, he would not enjoy it. He would cut the legs off a grasshopper and watch it try to jump around. It was really creepy. It was all a matter of power."

Thankfully, Ben didn't enjoy the same things and didn't get into this pattern of destructive behaviour. But on top of being dyslexic and green-red colour-blind, young PJ had a speech impediment. As a child he pronounced certain sounds with a noticeable lisp. Because of all these differences, Ben was constantly bullied.

There were other incidents. At one point, although Ben didn't remember what he had done, an employee at the orphanage hit him with the end of the vacuum cord, over and over.

PJ: The little metal prongs hit me and actually stuck in my back. The guy started freaking out because he was worried that it was going to be stuck there. I reached back and I pulled it out and said, "What? You don't like hitting me when it's stuck in my back?" and I was laughing. That was the last time I cried or showed emotion or let someone get to me. There was another situation. Another employee had cornered me in some room and he was telling me to take my pants down. That was creepy and weird! I ended up hitting him in the face with a plastic fork and I ran away. What a fucking douche! Trying to tell me to take my pants down.... What is wrong with you!

NF: Were you afraid that man was going to try to punish you somehow?

PJ: The punishment was this dude trying to touch me with my pants down! What would be the other punishment? Get put on timeout? At least you are not touching me with my pants down. I feel like victims look like victims. Like I can walk into a lineup and pick the guy who gets bullied. I was not going to be that victim.

Ben was just a kid. A kid who loved comic books about superheroes. A kid in an orphanage where many children were going the wrong way. And he, too, followed that path. The kids would break into cars and look at the car's airbag models. They would then write down the streets where the cars were parked and sell the information in exchange for candy.

But things were about to change. When Ben was almost 10 years old, a woman from Seattle visited the orphanage looking to adopt. Her husband had passed away, and she had inherited a large sum of money. Ben gave her a tour of the orphanage while introducing her to the kids. She was particularly interested in two little boys. Ben was old enough to know that his chances for being adopted were rather low and diminishing the older he got.

"Once you hit 10, you are there for the long haul. When people show up to adopt, you show them all the young cool kids and the babies because you don't usually get adopted at 10, especially if you're a boy. I had already made up my mind that I wasn't going to get adopted."

During the visit, Ben told the woman about the other boys, as well as himself: how he got there, where he came from, and so on. "She didn't take a look at the kids, and she just left. I thought it was strange," said PJ.

It was him she had in mind.

For the first time in his life he had spending money and was pampered by a caring mother. His new mother had many other adopted children. Many of them were like Ben's peers at the orphanage — directionless and looking for trouble. But Ben avoided their negative influence.

"The other kids got in a lot more trouble than I did," said PJ, "because they would sneak out at night. I would just say, 'You know what, Mom? I'm going out.' She would say, 'Don't go out!' and I would respond, 'I'm hearing what you're saying, but I'm just not going to listen. She would say, 'You're on timeout!' And I would say, 'Okay, over in my room on my Xbox.' When you go from a place that is so terrible to a place that is just amazing, it doesn't matter how much they try to make it terrible; it still is amazing. The best times I had in Texas don't even compare to the worst times I've had in Seattle."

By his 12th birthday he had become interested in volunteering for various causes. He was developing an interest in social issues. By 16, he was volunteering with the neighbourhood watch. At his high school, Ben was still bullied. But he was also a skilled fighter by then, having trained in martial arts from the time he relocated to Seattle. By 14 he already had a black belt.

"I have been a champion athlete in every sport I've touched," he said, "and part of that was because I was thrown away by my parents and I felt like I had to show my new one that she had made the right choice. I don't think it is okay to become a criminal just because you grew up in the ghetto. If you're dedicated, the results will come out."

Ben had a major growth spurt when he was 15 or 16. Combined with his vigorous training, he had a chance to change the script. He promised himself he wasn't going to be a victim anymore.

"I came back to school for what was probably the worst six months for the bullies," said PJ. "My principal sat down with me and explained to me that bullies lead on fear. On my end, I wouldn't punch people in the face, but they would flinch. She didn't know what I was. She was saying that I was something different than a bully, and she said that something really bad was going to happen to me if I didn't stop this. I wasn't intimidating them like they would do to me. I was hurting them.

"For example, I was in the bathroom and a guy grabbed me by my feet and lifted me upside down. The guys pretended that they were going to put my head into the toilet bowl, so I put my hand up and they were never able to do it. They felt that it was funny. But when I came back, I waited for the guy until he was walking to the urinal. I walked up behind him and just started to pee on him. He turned around and looked me in the face, and I just socked him in the face. He landed on the ground and I rubbed his face in the urine and walked away. At some point, the principal stepped in for good and said, 'You can't do that.'"

PJ said he was interested in intimidating the people who harassed him, but he actually hurt them. "If you believe you are right," he explained, "even if you are wrong, that is just as dangerous. And I was 100 percent sure that these bullies were torturing me — when in reality they were not torturing me, they were just teasing me, and I took it very seriously."

The school principal certainly could have recognized that Ben was also being picked on. When the other boys tried to intimidate him by threatening to hold his head in the toilet, that was bullying. The rough treatment by his classmates led to isolation. Ben avoided eating in the cafeteria because it was harder to protect himself there. He chose instead to eat alone in more isolated parts of the school, like the library. When the principal told Ben that he was going to be in real trouble, she also explained that he was really hurting people as his level of training gave him the potential to inflict serious harm on his tormentors.

"Bullies are just mean-spirited kids," PJ told me. "Because I lived with criminals, I could rationally think out consequences from a very young age. I didn't care about what happened to the people, but I cared about the consequences. So at 11, my [adoptive] mother would tell me, 'You have to eat your mashed potatoes, or you'll never get your vegetables.' And I would sit and think, 'Okay … if I were to break it up into blocks, the mashed potatoes would be about 15 separate blocks. No, thank you. I am just going to walk it off, because it is a battle I am losing. It's three blocks of veggies for 15 blocks of potatoes. Why would I play that game?' And I have felt like that my whole life. So when I got to high school and we were doing bad things, others would be embarrassed or say they didn't do it. But my principal would ask me if I did it and I would say, 'Absolutely. He deserved it.' She had never met anyone like that."

Although people continued to bully him until he was 16, PJ said it began to taper off. Bullies, after all, want easy prey, and Ben was proving to be more difficult to assault as he grew stronger and more self-assured. Eventually Ben graduated from high school and received a full college scholarship for bowling.

But Ben wasn't interested in school. He was becoming someone else. He was becoming Phoenix Jones.

10

SALT LAKE CITY

After my eventful and enlightening time spent in Seattle, I took a twenty-hour bus ride to my next destination. When I got there, I felt as if I had been transported to another world. Salt Lake City was beautiful, surrounded by some of the highest mountains in the country. Although the city was much smaller than I expected, the green scenery won me over. As I left the bus terminal, I got a cab and went right to my hotel. Two things made Utah particularly appealing: one, the Black Monday Society was there, and although I did not think they were as active as other groups, they were interesting people to interview; and two, it was also the home of the supervillain group the Roaming Eye of Doom. And since I wanted to interview at least one group of supervillains, what better opportunity to go to a city where there are RLSHs to interview as well!

The Black Monday Society was unique. Their look was darker and more sinister than other groups. They wear scary-looking masks and black leather. In a way, they reminded me of a cross between a Halloween party and a thrash metal band. I came to find that a lot of their style comes heavily from the influence of the group's founder, Insignis, now called Nihilist, otherwise known as Dave Montgomery. He chooses not to hide his identity but uses his Black Monday Society persona as a symbol for what he is trying to do. Formerly from Detroit, Michigan, the tattoo-parlour owner has always had a desire to buck conventional thinking and inspire others to do the same. The Black Monday Society operates differently and has different goals than the other teams I had met with. I thought of them as arch-individualists within a community of individualists.

On the other end of the spectrum, the RLSV group the Eye of Doom was interesting in a different way. At that point in time, their actual home in Salt Lake City, Utah, was a closely guarded secret. Their social media pages all stated they were from places other than Utah. The actual whereabouts of the "evil" entertainers was a point of conjecture and speculation for many in the Real Life Super Hero Facebook world. Personal information and images were fiercely protected, and for good reason, I would soon find out. Not even the Black Monday Society knew that the renowned villain group was operating in their own city. In fact, both teams had met on at least two occasions, a situation that the BMS would only learn at a future date, much to the amusement of the online community.

Even though I found the BMS interesting, making the trip just for them probably wasn't the best use of my time. I was mainly interested in the Eye of Doom. I had mentioned my planned visit to Salt Lake City to the Golden Don, but he wasn't all that enthusiastic at first. I remember one of his messages, "Sure, we may be funny and entertaining in a half-assed way, but we don't actually DO anything. Don't get me wrong, we do a lot more than most of the 'heroes' out there, but compared to the people YOU met? We are just jokers." I understood where he was coming from, as he was referring to the various personalities I had been interviewing, but I told him that his group made more of an impact than they thought. He deferred to the Baroness, who also expressed the same concerns that the Don did. I told her that the Eye affects the RLSH world far more than they may realize. RLSHs use Facebook to communicate, and most people in that world listen to the Eye of Doom. Some hate them and some love them, but everyone knows they hold RLSHs accountable for their actions. I again used the "internal affairs" analogy to describe how I saw their role in the superhero community.

I finally convinced them to meet with me and assured them I wouldn't be disappointed. Kaptain Blackheart of the Roaming Eye of

Doom even pointed out that after all my encounters with superheroes, I probably had more patrol experience than most of the self-described superheroes out there.

The day after my arrival I started to prepare for my patrol with the Black Monday Society.

At the hotel, I met Red Voltage, Dave Montgomery, and Asylum, three tall men, including one — Red Voltage — who was quite young. Dave Montgomery is hard not to recognize due to his facial tattoos. Aside from his charming smile, they are the first thing someone would notice. His ink documents years of his life, and two of his tattoos were actually done by his six-year-old daughter.

Dave, the laid-back Real Life Super Hero, created the BMS in 2006. He had just quit drinking on his doctor's orders. He was bored and needed a purpose in his life. Like most RLSHs, he was a lifelong fan of superheroes and had drawn them for as long as he could remember. He found out about Mr. Silent and Dr. Discord in Indiana. Dave reached out to them via email and was immediately on his journey to superhero-dom.

I asked Dave where he got the idea for his group's name. "Everyone hates Mondays. So we take somebody's bad day and turn it around for them. That's what we're there to do. The Black Monday Society just sounded right and it rang well."

He created personas to be a symbol, but he never felt like he had to hide. "There's more strength in people in knowing who you are and what you do. I never hid my name. Power to the people! The more people know about you, the more support you get. I'm a tattoo artist. You think anyone is dumb enough to knock me off? Do you know how many people would be pissed? I tattoo bikers, bad guys — I tattoo everybody."

He and Ghost, who wasn't with us that day, were the first members. At first the costumes were not very elaborate. Dave's consisted of a gas mask, a fedora hat, and a raincoat.

"I remember the first time." Dave recalled. "We told each other, 'It's okay, dude. If anyone asks, this is a college experiment.' That was just in case anyone would freak out on us because we were walking around with masks. And it was addicting at first. It was kind of cool. Nothing really bad happened, so we started getting more elaborate into the costumes, and I started getting into costuming, mask making, and armour making."

As I have said before, I could see the addictive nature of this hobby. For many, the feeling of power stemming from defending others was a major factor. The potential of danger gives superheroes surges of adrenalin. In Dave's case, he described it as the same rush he got from drinking. It was the thing that took him out of his everyday life. He said he also likes the idea of helping people anonymously. It took his personal ego out of the equation. "Your persona becomes a whole different identity. It becomes a different person altogether. So when you slip into the character that you created for yourself, you don't have the same problems as you do in everyday life."

As an alcoholic, he felt he did not have much of a personality. So he portrayed his former self, in a sense, by wearing all black and calling himself Nihilist. To him, it was a form of renewal. "That is why I like the Real Life Super Hero movement and why I am not a cop. I respect the cops doing what they do — it's great — but the system itself is broken. I say screw it all and start fresh! As superheroes, we start fresh from our own moral decency. It's new. It is not tainted. That's why I can't stand people putting rules to all of this stuff. It drives me insane. Just let it be what it is, and let your old moral decisions guide you on the street. It's new. It's the beauty of it all."

On his patrols, he has been approached by all manner of people — cops, drunks, addicts, gang members — but his calm confidence lets others know he is not a threat. He worked on many different ways of presenting himself until ultimately choosing Insignis. He wanted to be a symbol. He put his mind to it and spent nearly $5,000 to create his latex costume from scratch. He also developed and streamlined techniques so he could help others create costumes as well. He has had several looks over the years, some moulded in latex, others formed and cut from leather. He created his current mask, formed from heat-contoured impact-resistant ABS plastic. He also makes masks for heroes outside his team, like the California Initiative's NightBug.

His team fluctuates in membership, sometimes five, sometimes twelve, but the core is strong: Ghost, Asylum, Foolking, Oni, Professor Midnight, and himself. Being a single father, Dave has to take care of his little one at night, meaning he's had to slow down since he had his daughter. Eventually he passed the leadership to another member.

"That's when I gave up leadership to Red Voltage, so I can just be the old man in the backdrop. I could just be another soldier on the street, and I won't take away from the hierarchy of the team. Somebody always has to be the bright leader. No better guy in the world than Red Voltage for the task.

"Okay, humility is really the greatest power of all. It really is. If you treat everyone you meet like a king, it doesn't matter how they treat you. The more humble you are, the more power you gain. Well, I humbled myself … boom … Red Voltage is leader. I can easily handle that. I'll take an order from him. Even though I'm the guy in the background, still putting things together, he can call the shots. It's best for the team."

He got his humility from his mother. When he grew up, back in Detroit, his father was a stern truck driver in the Teamsters Union, and his mother was a free-spirited "little French chick." "Dad was strict, and Mom was very loving and caring. Dad was always 'uphold yourself in the highest respect,' 'always be clean' — three-hour lectures on how to properly butter your toast and not lick the knife, crap like that. My mom taught me the power of humility. So between the two of them, I became what I am today."

Now in his early 40s, Dave has been a tattoo artist for over 20 years. He's drawn all his life and turned his passion into his livelihood. "It's easy to get carried away tattooing people. Sometimes they feed your ego and tell you how wonderful you are, and then they give you money to hurt them so you think, 'Wow! I must be great!' So you get that little rock-star attitude, and I try to keep that in check just because it is better. I went through a time where I wasn't so humble. That was after my first marriage went bad. It was a whole scenario. I started tattooing outside of Detroit, and I got mean and very vicious."

He had a change of perspective when he moved to Utah. He travelled America for over eight years, setting up tattoo shops. He taught people the profession and considered it a mutual learning experience. "I ended up coming to Utah and I fell in love with the state. I don't know why. I think because it is a 1950s retarded bubble. You can do anything you want here and get away with it. All you got to do is be that much smarter than anyone else, and it works. I do it great. So I really loved the state. It is just one of those things. I wanted to be a little bit nicer and a little kinder because I was actually happy here. I was happy for the first time in a long time."

He was setting up the tattoo parlour in Utah for his daughter. It's even named after her. At the age of five, she tattooed her dad for the first time.

His perspective started to skew when he was young. He learned he was charming and could manipulate people easily. "When I was a kid, it was so easy to tell people what they wanted. Anything from girls, when I discovered sex, game on. I think I slept with my entire graduating class, to be honest with you. It was pretty bad and then there was the class before and after. You just tell them what they want to hear. I was dabbling lightly into drugs. Mostly just marijuana," Dave said.

While he never had any chronic drug addictions, he did spiral into an unhealthy cycle with alcohol. "I drank a little bit in high school," he recalled. "I could outrun the past if I was chasing down the bottle. It worked for a while. But after some time, it grows old and you want something more. I was 26. I was 210 pounds. I was fat and bloated. It actually gave me hyperglycemia. I drank so much and damaged my body so much that I actually became ill. And that is when I realized that I was not ready to give up quite yet. I didn't want to die. So it probably helped start the whole anxiety attack thing. Everything changed in my life."

Today he has four children, including one daughter who passed away during childbirth. He gave both his daughters names based on men's names to set them up for power and respect. His desire for power and respect may have been the reason some have criticized him for founding the BMS for attention. He responded to that criticism: "I do it for the reaction. I want to see what you do. I like to see people squirm sometimes. I don't go out on patrol as much to help others really as to help me. It's for me. If people don't like it? Fine. Just try to stop me."

In a way, he's one of those RLSHs who understood that patrolling is really for him because he's the one who really needs it. He hopes someone might try to stop him, if only for the rush. He said he would rather die a hero's death than die of old age, relying on others to care for him. If he dies young, he believes his kids would be okay. "Because I've already left two children and they came out amazing. That is how I know. The impact that we want to leave on people's lives and the impact we think we leave are two different things. It takes away a lot of ego. Humble yourself and be real."

Many children are denied the influence of a loving parent. In regard to the potential for serious effect on them, Dave Montgomery provides this advice:

"Take control and be somebody. For someone who can't stand victims, I certainly like helping them. I'm willing to see them aspire to something more. "

⚡

Next it was time to interview Asylum. Asylum is one of the core members of the Black Monday Society. Having carefully selected his name, he had been thinking of a dual meaning: the first, of course, being a place for the insane; and the second, a place one can go for security and safety. He feels that both sides depict the light and dark sides of his life. He thinks of himself as a force for good. He describes what he does as a member of the BMS as being a member of a citizen's patrol. The Black Monday Society provides a gimmick to get people's attention. He contends that one does not need a mask or a cape to go out and do something. He simply states that their job as the BMS is to remind people that good can be done. They have also been known to provide aid to those in need. He feels like he needs to give back to the community he has taken from.

He does admit, however, that the BMS's frightening appearance has the potential to intimidate some members of the public. But everyone on the team knows not to let their costumes get in the way of the fact that they are just regular people out to help. Their image makes them more visible, but the look itself is not the point. When they are in costume, more people will stop to talk to them. Some giggle. When they first started patrolling, people would cross the street to avoid them. Now that they have been featured in local media stories, regular people are more aware of their purpose. Sometimes they are given information, like where car break-ins are happening. That way they can go be a presence in the affected area in an effort to help discourage crime. Their presence and image may make someone think twice about committing a crime.

Asylum met Dave Montgomery while he was working at a club where Dave's ex-wife worked. While Dave was drawing at the bar, Asylum struck up a conversation about comic books. Dave mentioned that he was trying to recruit someone with Asylum's build so he could create a suit for them.

"I brushed it off in passing until my fiancée, who was a bartender at that club, told me that guy actually had a superhero team," Asylum said. "I thought it was a joke, but that night I could not get the idea out of my head."

The next time he saw Dave, he started his tattoo apprenticeship. "Dave is the one that taught me how to tattoo. I've been tattooing with Dave for about five and a half years. About two weeks after my apprenticeship, I actually went out on patrol. So my tattoo life and my superhero life actually go hand and hand with each other, and it all started directly from Dave," Asylum recalled.

Asylum had been practising martial arts since he was four years old. He got better and better as he got older, but he got bored. He had a beautiful family life. They went to church and were close. But the older he got, the more trouble he tried to get into. It didn't help that he didn't feel that school made much sense for him. "The trouble that I got into when I was a teenager had nothing to do with my parents. They were all my stupid mistakes." Stealing cars, selling drugs, violence. Through a mix of criminal and martial arts connections, he had an opportunity to study Muay Thai as well as jiu jitsu.

While he was still in junior high, Asylum severely injured his knee, and the injury kept him from pursuing sports in a traditional sense. He started participating in criminal activities, like selling drugs or collecting money that was owed to him or to others. He also started hanging out with dangerous people and stopped going to school. He recalled being at several parties where guns were present. He was often the youngest person at the party, but he was accepted and recruited by older criminals. He would never carry a gun, however, even during a high-stakes drug transaction.

"I think about the death wish thing: if anything happens, sweet, I get shot, then it's done. I don't have to worry about it. We did things from little collections and selling coke, to collecting twenty or thirty thousand dollars from people, and if you don't have the money, I break a leg and take your car."

As you can imagine, sometimes the clientele that owes money to drug dealers is less than reliable. Asylum would resort to various methods to get his point across: "I wear a mask as a superhero, and I wore a mask when I was on the other side. I used to have a big hockey mask with a big smiley face on it. It was creepy and weird, but it hid my identity as much as I wanted it to."

He realized he needed to get out of the life he was living when he had to identify the body of his friend at the morgue. It really struck home for him and gave him a different perspective on his life. He gave up all his financial and criminal affiliations. "I knew that either I had to get out, make a deal to get out, or I was the next one on the slab," he said.

At age 31, the self-proclaimed big-hearted hero states he is far beyond those teenage years. "I have no doubts in who I am and what my abilities are because of those years. I had to make peace with myself so many times with the way that I lived that what I am now is solidified 100 percent. I know exactly the man I am and there is no question about it."

These days, as a member of the Black Monday Society, he spends his time and talents to better the world he lives in, instead of making it worse. He feels he has a lot to atone for.

"There is no vigilante inside the Black Monday Society. We don't run around beating people. It's not our job to decide who is guilty and who's innocent. We are there for an extra set of ears and an extra set of eyes for the police."

He states it's a huge personal decision to be a member of the BMS. The team size can fluctuate for many reasons in his opinion: "Some guys are just scared. They are afraid of the repercussions, [thinking] that we are going to get shot or stabbed. Some guys get out there and they feel stupid. They are about the 'girls love me,' and when they put a suit on, nobody knows who they are and people are yelling stuff at them from a car. They call them freaks and tell them it's not Halloween. They want to do good, but they just can't do it the way that we do it. They have to find something else to do, like charity work or volunteering somewhere, which is great! If you are willing to help out your community and do something, then that is awesome. If we can inspire you to help anybody, then we've done our part. Most of us never started this thing to get any acclaim for it. We never wanted the press and there are a couple of guys on the team that avoid the press."

Although Salt Lake City doesn't have as much violence as many other cities in the United States, bad things still happen. Asylum recounted a story where a young woman was intoxicated and got kicked out of her boyfriend's car. While on patrol, they found her and helped her get to the train station so she could go to her friend's house. She did not have any shoes on and may have been more than drunk. While the team was protecting and escorting her, many men made lewd and lascivious offers to "buy her." They even offered money to the girl directly. The RLSHs could tell she was not in a position to make the best choices, but they knew they could not control her choices. They politely reminded her that she wanted to be safe and get to her friend's house. Asylum joked about what it must have looked like on the commuter train that night: a barefoot drunk girl and the Black Monday Society.

Maybe more than through his efforts on patrol, Asylum tries to make a difference by influencing young people in his daily life. He knows first-hand of the ripple effect that one person's bad decisions can have in the lives of many people. He noticed a teen cousin heading in the same direction as he did when he was young. He had a heart-to-heart discussion with him, trying to impress upon him that it's never just one person who is affected by the choices he makes.

It was time to patrol. The BMS were supposed to be a larger group that night, but there were only three of us. No one else wanted to go out. I met with Red Voltage, the current leader, and a new member, Flame Wing, a young man who wanted to become a police officer and who was studying in the field. We patrolled around the streets of Salt Lake City. Red Voltage waved at people and two police officers asked to take pictures with us, but nothing else happened. The SLC streets are relatively quiet. Perhaps that is why the BMS only patrol for an hour, each weekend. Yet they have still had national attention for their efforts and were featured in the HBO documentary.

⚡

The next day I was finally going to meet with the villains. This would be my first time interviewing RLSVs in person. But it wasn't like interviewing serial killers; I wasn't nervous. I knew by now they were just regular people.

We all met at the hotel. The supervillains looked exactly as they did in their pictures, but with bigger smiles. Aside from the Golden Don, none were really tall. After all the emails we had exchanged, I felt like I already knew them. One thing was for sure: aside from the fact he looked nothing like his mask, something about the Golden Don intrigued me, but I couldn't say exactly what.

The Real Life Super Hero movement definitely reached a new level when the HBO documentary was released. Many RLSHs did not connect with civilians prior to that time. The villains I met with in Utah had all seen the documentary: Kaptain Blackheart, a 35-year-old man; his fiancée, the Baroness; his cousin, Professor Plague; and his best friend, the Golden Don.

The Golden Don said he was both amazed and distressed when he saw the film. To this group of supervillains, the actions of the superheroes depicted in the movie ranged from improbable, to preposterous, to unsettling. Some superheroes showcased in the documentary, he felt, seemed to be deranged or delusional. Indeed, one of the superheroes in the documentary appeared to be an alcoholic who believed he was the voice of God. Another one looked like a compulsive hoarder. The superhero team from Salt Lake City looked terrifying. Some RLSHs didn't even have training of any kind. Kaptain explained that he became a Real Life Super Villain because of his disappointment and disillusionment with the RLSH movement. This was even before he came to know them as individuals. When he heard rumours about costumed crime fighters, he had hoped that his childhood dreams may be realized; however, reality proved to be less than he hoped. Some seemed earnest and genuine, and some seemed dangerous.

"We knew they could not be stopped in a way that an actual villain or criminal would do it," said Kaptain Blackheart. "We had to finesse it. We figured we would freak some people out and see what happened. Why? They did not deserve the title. I was kind of let down a little bit. I felt like if those guys were fake — some of the biggest guys in the country were supposedly in my state and they were Mickey Mouse.... If they were, then there's probably a pretty good chance that they are all Mickey Mouse."

Then he explained that the Baroness contacted a RLSH who was located in her city, but not related to the Black Monday Society. Kaptain Blackheart continued: "We found one local guy that played the game. He had a profile on Facebook. We're not saying his name because he was completely a joke. But he was supposedly a Real Life Super Hero and he was new. He was trying to get as many friends as he could possibly get, so we just started communicating with him. He had a 'hotline' you could call him on if anything went down, but he did not have a car. He said he carried a sword and other ninja gear."

Much to the surprise of Kaptain Blackheart and the Golden Don, the Baroness, who previously was mainly a spectator to the online exchanges, was more than willing to call the hotline and talk with the samurai-themed

RLSH. The Golden Don jumped in on the conversation: "Kap came up with the name for her [the Baroness] as 'Sally Smash' on the spot and it stuck. So we improvised a fake Real Life Super Hero team named Lake Town Vigilantes. Having a lady on the team had added a high degree of credibility to the situation. When approaching another group, if a woman is involved, it makes the communication more relaxed, as there is no ego or competition, like sometimes with men. She had him eating out of the palm of her hand — I think because he was hoping in the back of his mind they would go on patrol alone or something. Either way, we had already 'outgrown' him before we were off the phone."

So they created a hero team. The Baroness — of course — was Sally Smash; Kaptain Blackheart was Mistery; and the Golden Don was Dr. Thornhill. They took pictures in dark costumes they pieced together from various Halloweens for their Facebook profiles and tried to look ominous and mysterious. With Sally Smash/the Baroness being the ambassador of the team, and all of them working together to build a substantial online presence, it was easy to make an impact in a short time. The Baroness received many unsolicited advances.

"Right after activating my Facebook page as Sally Smash," she said, "I was immediately bombarded by men who called themselves RLSHs with messages that were completely derogatory and sexually explicit. It was an absolutely horrible experience for me. It was probably consistent for about three months before I got a reputation for being a bitch. And they kind of laid off of me a little bit, but I was so put out because it was the exact opposite of what a superhero is supposed to be. That is not okay, and it's harassment. From my perspective, they think they can do anything because they hide behind their masks, but it doesn't make it okay. If you are going to call yourself a superhero, you better damn well act like one."

The Golden Don said: "There is a quote from author John Wooden that states: 'The true test of a man's character is what he does when no one is watching.' This would seem to hold true for the many who have claimed RLSH status, except it would be modified in this context as: 'A person's true identity is revealed when he wears a mask.'

"We got a good response as the Lake Town Vigilantes," he continued. "We represented ourselves as vaguely dangerous costumed crimefighters. We said we carried weapons on patrol. Before we knew it, we had contact with heroes and teams who we thought would never talk to us. It was brilliant and fun. Unless you are a *real* RLSH, being in the RLSH online community is just a game, and one of the biggest indicators of how well you are playing is how many friends you can get. You can get 250 friends in less than a week if you want, easily."

The group was at a crossroads. They weren't sure what they would do with their involvement in this phenomenon. During one of their meetings they brought up the possibility of actually becoming a hero team or just quitting and moving on, but they agreed that they were having too much fun to walk away completely. They acknowledged the hypocrisy of wanting to stay in an environment they originally wanted to eliminate.

The Golden Don continued: "While on one of my forays in the field, I talked to a hero from Florida, the Purple Lotus. He sent me a picture he had drawn of Dr. Thornhill. It was quick and simple, but very powerful. It looked like a vintage comic book panel. As a result, we chatted for a while. I played my part, but he was sincere and truly seemed to have a genuine desire to help people. I had to take a moment to re-evaluate what I was doing. I wasn't going to be a hero in real life. I was being a fake hero because I did not respect RLSHs and thought they were all phony. But it turned out there were some — a few — good and genuine people. The Purple Lotus even gave me his phone number and asked me to text him. I didn't, but it made me think. We discussed this as a team and all agreed we wanted to stay in the superhero world but wanted to do it on our terms and to be true to ourselves."

Around this time the Baroness had yet again been inappropriately propositioned on the Internet, but this time by someone who did not call himself a hero. She learned how to publicly humiliate him by performing what she called a "copy/paste/post," where she took a screen shot of what the offender said and posted it on her wall, sometimes tagging several friends in the image to ensure distribution. In response she was contacted by a Real Life Super Villain. He explained to her that the person who was harassing her was a troll and not a villain. He explained that a RLSV was a person who acts as a counterweight to the heroes and makes them accountable for any misdeeds.

For the four friends of Salt Lake City, this concept was food for thought. Being villains would serve their purpose. The soon-to-join Professor Plague was interested in hearing about the happenings in the RLSH world, and being "evil" would give him a place on the team. Sally Smash/the Baroness started networking with other Real Life Super Villains.

She met Octavius Fong (an evil puppet) online. He is also the leader of a group he created called the Roaming Eye of Doom. These new villains wanted in.

> Professor Plague (PP): Everyone wanted to expand their brand of superheroism to what they [the Eye] were doing. Which was awesome, but then it got to a point where, 'what else were they going to do?' We kind of saw that about 99 percent of these people were ridiculous; they were delusional and not many of them seemed to actually be going on patrol. It seemed like they stayed on the Internet. So we found this puppet who was talking bad about everyone on YouTube. Before this, we would look at the villains and we thought these guys were crazier than the heroes. It was just very confusing. The first Fong video that I ever saw was about a woman superhero who had done porn movies. He outted her by making a video on YouTube and showing it to the world. That was interesting and productive, so we thought maybe we should become villains.
>
> The Baroness (B): She does awesome work. The problem is she is a porn star! We thought about her going to visit the kids that had cancer in the hospitals and the parents finding out what else she does. That is a horrible thing, and I'm sure the parents would just be mortified. That is a big black mark on the community. Not that I have a problem with it — if that's what you choose to do with your life, that is 100 percent your choice, but ... they don't mix. It's like water and oil. So that is really what pushed us over the edge. It brought us to the conclusion that somebody needed to hold them accountable.
>
> Kaptain Blackheart (KB): Fong is one of the oldest villains that the community has. He was in the community before it was on Facebook. He could say whatever he wanted

because he was a puppet and he wasn't real. Of course, he was the most hated guy in that world.

The Golden Don (GD): Tom Fury [the hand controlling Octavius Fong] called himself the leader of the Eye. When filming, the puppet would call Tom "Boy," even though he was controlled by Tom. He had a great slogan: "All Hail the Eye!"This was said with much emphasis while pulling down the lower eyelid. It was very catchy and we all loved it. The Baroness worked a deal: once we had proven ourselves, we would actually become the Eye of the Roaming Eye of Doom. It became a mini-phenomenon. Because of our wit and charm and general "assholitude," we got heroes and villains alike hailing the Eye in videos and pictures. What was classic about it is that even though we were a powerful presence, we had a puppet for a boss. It was a riot.

Their reach was far beyond what they had planned, but now they had to find a balance. They had originally wanted to crush the RLSH world. Now they were becoming part of it. Those whom they had once despised were becoming their audience. The next step was to create individual personas. That was a task they did not take lightly, and they expected it to be an ongoing project. Fong wanted to make an announcement as soon as possible. He told the four that he had never encountered a group or individual talented enough to merit an invitation to join the Eye. The Baroness continued to be the point of contact with Fong in order to keep things less complicated. Kaptain Blackheart explained: "Six months on the Internet is like a year and a half in the real world. A lot of interaction happens on the Internet. Way more than in real life, and with people from all over. There were people in the villain game who we considered 'old school' and they were only on six months before us. So time is of the essence. Memories are short. If you're not right up in their faces, people forget."

I asked them about the origins of their personas and where they saw themselves in the group and the RLSH world.

As a self-proclaimed geek, Kaptain Blackheart grew up loving comic books, like many in the Real Life Super Hero community. He admired the action and nobility of the characters. He was thrilled by their conviction and the passion to do what they thought was right. He always longed for a sense of adventure and excitement. The pursuit of travel and danger even led him to join the United States Marine Corps.

He admits he had a short-sighted, youthful mindset: "I wanted to get shot at. That was my number one thing. I wanted bullets flying and dust bursting from the sandbag barricades." He went on to explain. "I really liked the idea. I felt like I won the lottery with all of my buddies, 'travelling the globe and meeting interesting people and trying to blow them up,' or whatever the slogan is. I thought that would be a cool adventure for me to do. I was not planning to go to college and I wasn't really ready to be a grown-up. I wanted something that I could look back on and go, 'that was crazy!'"

But the glamour soon faded for Blackheart as the reality of being in the military became apparent. While on manoeuvres in the Los Angeles National Forest, a comrade and close friend of his fell to his death in a ravine. Because they shared the same last name, he had felt a kinship with the fallen soldier. Initially, when the military families heard there was a death, the military only released the last name of the deceased lance corporal. When Blackheart's parents heard the name, they assumed it was their son who had died. Though they were relieved to learn their son was still alive, their hearts were heavy for the family who had lost their son. Blackheart brought the body home to the family and was a pallbearer at this marine's funeral. To this day, Blackheart has kept the jacket of his fallen friend, still stained with blood from that tragic day.

Kaptain Blackheart never cared much for authority and chose not to make the Marines his career. After his four-year commitment to the service, he attended film school in Los Angeles. He came up with a plot for a movie, and it was even optioned by a major movie studio, but ultimately nothing came of it, and he eventually moved back to Salt Lake City to be closer to his family.

His foray into the world of supervillainy happened quite suddenly. Before he knew it, he had become Kaptain Blackheart. When asked where his inspiration came from for the persona, he stated, "Kaptain Blackheart comes from Howard Pile's *Book of Pirates*. It's basically the history of the golden age of piracy. I am related to a famous pirate — the real me. *Kaptain Blackheart* is just me talking in a silly accent and saying what I want." Blackheart wears a black tricorne hat, a captain's coat, and black steampunk goggles that cover his eyes. He portrays a lovable hothead drunkard who constantly threatens to "Release the Kraken!"

As we talked, I asked him which RLSHs he thought were legitimate. The conversation turned toward Phoenix Jones, and Kaptain Blackheart continued: "I think it's taking a huge risk, and I don't think they should do it. You're going to get yourself hurt really bad or maybe somebody else. Let's say you run up and you're breaking up a fight and you push a guy and he takes two steps back into traffic and gets hit by a bus. Are you responsible for that? Would that have happened if you did not go and run into the situation? But really, Phoenix Jones is trying to do something good. But I think there are better and safer ways to make a difference. I hope nothing bad has to happen to make some people realize it."

While the Golden Don was listening and sometimes nodding, he was far from the imposing figure he appeared to be in costume. When dressed as a RLSV, he wears a hood to cover his head. He either wears a suit with a gold tie, or robes like a monk. His face is covered by a gold-coloured mask contorted in an angry frown. As he talks, the lower part of the jaw on the mask moves, creating a rather disturbing effect. Visually he could be best described like Dr. Doom from Marvel Comics; however, this is a comparison he likes to avoid. He'll extensively explain the differences if the issue is raised. At first I was uncomfortable when I saw him with his mask on. The other villains' masks at least showed parts of their faces. But the Golden Don's mask had its desired effect — at least on me!

Another aspect of the Don's persona is the mobster-style accent he employs when performing in videos and, most notably, during their call-in webcast radio show. The show became popular among those in the RLSH community. Heroes stay on hold for a long time, waiting for a chance to speak with the hosts, the Golden Don and Kaptain Blackheart. It's only a 30-minute show, and some RLSHs have complained that it isn't long enough. The heroes wanted these villains to have a longer show.

I had called in once, just to bug them and see how they would react to my fake persona, a dumb woman. They were actually very courteous and nice to the character I'd created.

All of the members of this team had strong personalities, especially Kaptain Blackheart and the Baroness. They carried their charisma over to the characters they created.

Next the Golden Don explained the creation of his persona: "No matter how much I wanted to take the time to craft a character, one came almost on a whim. The Golden Don is a play on the Hermetic Order of the Golden Dawn. It was a magical order in England during the late 19th and early 20th centuries. They practise rituals and spiritual development. It could be said it's one of the largest influences on the development of the occult in the modern world. Aleister Crowley was a member of the Golden Dawn and later went on to explore black magic. Some also say that Joseph Smith, the founder of the Mormon Church, was influenced by some of the same practises that established the Hermetic Order of the Golden Dawn. The 'don' reference is a joke added for 'Mafia Don.' That and the East Coast accent are a reference to organized crime. I usually contend that my gimmick is a reference to my opinion that religion is an organization based on fear, mystery, and magic."

The real person hiding behind the Golden Don was raised in a religious family with a reasonably strict level of discipline. He said he was from a generation where people still paddled their children. He was always a talented artist, but he had never felt like he had any direction. Part of this was due to a somewhat unstable home life. He states that his upbringing may have resulted in him needing validation and attention — something he has been able to get as a villain.

"I have this pocket response that I give to people," said the Golden Don. "It was actually a little gem Octavius Fong threw my way: 'We, at the Roaming Eye of Doom, are a group of like-minded individuals bent on world domination.' People are wondering what he's talking about. All of us have this perception that there are people who dress up in superhero costumes, and it's ridiculous. Even the most serious hero is absolutely preposterous.... So you'd better not take yourself too seriously because if you do, we will make fun of you. Folks who have proven themselves have nothing to fear from us."

He explained that the online RLSH world is driven by image.

"Image is all they have," said the Golden Don. "So if you can damage that, you can create fear. If someone's image is based on falsehood or inflated ego, it can be exploited. When someone oversteps their bounds, it may leave them open to retribution."

He says that in many ways, being a "good guy" is a trap because they can only operate within a certain range of acceptable behaviour. Whereas a villain, who may get less attention, will be able to do as they please with little criticism. That is not to say there are no conflicts among other villains, they just try to keep the conflicts from the eyes of the RLSHs. The Golden Don added, "If I had to break it down to one thing, one statement about being a Real Life Super Villain, it would be this: 'Real Life Super Villains are only as *evil* as Real Life Super Heroes are actually *heroes*.' Villains can't exist without heroes because they are created as a reflection of the preposterous nature of the RLSH movement."

A self-admitted "mean girl" growing up, the Baroness had her nickname before she was ever a villain. Kaptain Blackheart gave her the moniker because she reminded him of the dark haired femme fatale of the same name from the G.I. Joe comics, toys, and animated series. In many ways she serves as the intelligence officer for the Roaming Eye of Doom. Many people are more willing to open up to her than they are to the other members of the team. This may be because she is a woman, or maybe it's because she is the one member of the team who is willing to show her face.

The Baroness grew up in a good neighbourhood and went to a private school. She had everything she wanted. She was likely acting out because of the turmoil in her home life. As she got older, teen rebellion turned into poor choices. She spent time with the wrong people and fell into drugs. She was a victim of violence and abuse on more than one occasion. It became hard to hide her substance abuse from her parents. She was able to get clean when she became pregnant, but then she dealt with the difficulties of being a teen mother.

With help from the others, the Baroness spearheads involvement in events for charities like "Sub for Santa," and she recently took part in a fundraiser for a homeless shelter in partnership with the Kid Rock Foundation. She feels that helping the homeless is important but that it is more effective when the assistance is administered by professionals and agencies that are dedicated to helping the poor learn how to take care of themselves. She feels that a simple handout merely prolongs a homeless person's situation.

"Teenagers, and single parents, and the girls on the streets, just not feeling like you have anywhere to turn, I know what that feels like. So that's why I do what I do as far as the community outreach stuff. Now I've got a bachelor's degree in political science. I have an awesome job with awesome benefits. I'm 30 years old. If there is one bit of advice I can give to kids it's that they have to get an education."

She continued: "I wouldn't feel okay if I was making commentary on other people's charity work and I wasn't trying to do the same thing. I'm a commentator. I'm the judge and executioner. I try to let their peers be their jury, but I feel that everybody in the community needs to start being held accountable for their actions. It looks cool from the outside but once you're involved, it's different. I saw a lot of abuse of power. A lot of people with big names let their ego take over, and they said and did things that they probably wouldn't normally do, but they were feeling comfortable behind a mask. We saw both good and bad character in people.

"There are a few people that I have a lot of respect for and that I think are doing this for the right reasons. Like Rock N Roll: she is my favourite superhero. I really like NightBug and the whole California Initiative. Those guys are totally awesome. I think Purple Lotus and Agent Seven are as legit as they can be by calling themselves superheroes. They do it for the right reasons. And they're all very respectful. Those are the people that should be leaders in the community, that the newer members of the community should be looking up to.

"Instead they see crazy acts from people like the Ray, who I think was brave because he did what he thought was right, but that doesn't make it right. I have respect for Phoenix Jones and what he does. He's got actual training, and he has a team of people that he works with. He has really good leadership skills, from what I've seen. It's just as I said before, once you put that mask and costume on, you have to be above the stakes. You have to be aware of what you are doing at all times, because you are being watched. When we went out undercover with the Black Monday Society, we dressed in uniform, as militants, and were prepared for real things."

Wait … villains on patrol with heroes? It turns out part of the fun the Eye was having was continuing to pose as the Lake Town Vigilantes while they were carrying out villainy. Most of the time, villains relegate themselves to the Internet, never having direct contact with the heroes. The Roaming Eye of Doom wanted to change that. Red Voltage, the leader of the Black Monday Society, invited Sally Smash and the crew out on patrol. Not wanting to pass up an opportunity at villainy, the Eye dressed as militants and went on patrol in disguise. The Black Monday Society had no idea that the Lake Town Vigilantes were also the popular villain team the Eye of Doom. So the Eye met with the BMS and patrolled downtown Salt Lake City. At first, splitting up to meet up later to patrol the Occupy SLC encampment, the villains said they were going a different route, but they mostly spent the time sneaking around, giggling, and spying on the hero team. The Golden Don said, "Mostly I wanted to see if they were really doing anything."

Kaptain Blackheart said: "I just expected them to do more good and not just walk. Like pass out a blanket to somebody who was cold, or whatever. I gave a cigarette to a homeless guy. Red Voltage said that was like charity. I said I don't think that really counts. I said I am being very nice and giving a guy a cigarette, but that does not make me a superhero. In fact, I'm helping this guy die a little faster, if anything."

They had considered later revealing in a video a playful ambush on Red Voltage, but they decided against it. The Black Monday team was good-natured and did not claim to do anything more than "fight apathy." Interestingly enough, on the night of that patrol, Impact, a new trial member of the BMS was present. He only patrolled once, and for good reason. Later that week, he made sexual comments online to the Baroness about her breasts, not knowing that he was, in fact, sending messages to Sally Smash, with whom he had patrolled just a few nights before. She copy/paste/posted his private messages to her wall and criticized the BMS for letting a degenerate into their ranks. Red Voltage posted a video of apology to the Baroness. Dave Montgomery, the quasi-retired team founder also messaged the Baroness to expressly indicate that Impact was no longer a member of the BMS. This incident was fuel for entertainment and laughter for the villains. As time went on, they revealed the prank, letting it leak that the Lake Town Vigilantes were also the Roaming Eye of Doom.

With Professor Plague, it was different. He'd had a reasonably mundane upbringing. It was not without heartache and challenges. Plague's father passed away when he was 18 years old, but before that, for the most part, he had little to complain about. He always loved the concept of the mad scientist, and he enjoys research and analysis. He also gravitated to work in the medical field. He was always into comic books and science fiction.

However, there was another part of his personality that was a little harder to come to terms with. "I never cared about being different about the fact I was a geek, but when it came to being homosexual, I didn't want to be gay. I wanted to have a regular family. I wanted to grow up, get married, have a wife, have kids, and I held onto that for a very long time."

Coming to terms with his sexuality did not come quickly. It took him years of soul-searching and self-analysis. Thankfully, Professor Plague enjoys being analytical and used his mind to find acceptance for himself. He also has applied his critical thinking and observation skills to his perspective on the RLSH community. He does not interact as much with the RLSH world as the rest of his teammates, partly because his job requires him to work late nights.

Much of his energy and contribution to the team come through his performances in the Roaming Eye of Doom videos. "This video thing was completely new to us. We were totally amateurs. We started using my iPhone and the most simple editing software available that just comes on Windows."

Even in the beginning when the videos were rough, they were still funny and effective. Later on they became more complex. Plot lines were introduced and the Baroness would pore over the computer for hours, editing scenes together. The work paid off. The videos became part of the villain experience and impacted the way the RLSH community interacted with one another.

Professor Plague recalled, "When Silver Sentinel got married, we made a video where we made a poison cake. We were going to try to send it to him, and we were going to try to poison the whole wedding. We put that on the Internet, and he thought it was awesome. He loved it. Kaptain has a video where he makes fun of superheroes for being overweight, and what's funny about that is he's got a pretty good belly. He makes a joke that he is not the most fit man, but that some of the heroes make him look like David Beckham. He says, 'Put down the quarter-pounder ... pick up the ten-pounder,' as in a barbell. So with that kind of video, we don't call out one superhero, we make a statement about the community as a whole."

Through the satirical efforts of the Eye, many RLSHs started to relax and stopped taking themselves so seriously. Along with the fact that RLSVs were getting more attention, it also meant that RLSHs on the Internet did not feel like they had to posture as much. Professor Plague explained, "When we came along, we started to kind of bridge that gap between heroes, and it's interesting how many heroes respect us. But on the flipside, many heroes still hate us. We get on there to make a mockery of what they do, which is true to some extent. That is part of what we do."

Heroes and villains alike began to embrace the developing nature of the community. "That was something strange about being an RLSV before us — before the Eye — villains were pretty much portrayed as Internet bullies. They got on there, and they were mean to the heroes, and they said horrible things, and they got blocked really fast. A lot of the heroes would not give them the time of day."

Professor Plague took a step back to try to look at the big picture when it comes to seeing who he feels in the RLSH community is genuine. "On top of following what RLSHs do online, I will get on the Internet at work in the middle of the night, and I will just do a Google news search for RLSHs. But even if I don't have the opportunity to talk to a lot of them, the Baroness and the Golden Don are a little bit better at getting information out of someone. So a lot of my information comes second-hand from them."

He does see the irony in being accepted by RLSHs. He wishes there was more positive mentoring with new heroes and proper guidance for minors who would like to participate.

When it comes to youth, especially those like him who struggle with who they are, he is brief yet effective: "Just be who you are. Don't be afraid to be yourself."

⚡

I knew that meeting with these RLSVs would be a unique experience, but I did not have any preconceived notions. When in contact with the Golden Don, I put pressure on him to show me what they did. He said, "Well, you have been around the country and walked around with guys in pajamas all over the country. Now you get to see what the villains do for their 'patrol.'" The Roaming Eye of Doom, besides being known for their popular radio show, loved to make movies. They wrote a script for a 15-minute movie and cast me as the central character.

"Me?" I was nervous. My first reaction was to politely decline.

"What? You are not afraid to walk around in a bulletproof vest with weirdo RLSHs, but you are afraid to make a silly film with some weirdo RLSVs? Come on.... You did not come all the way out here for nothing, did you?" said the Golden Don.

I was initially concerned that the video might depict me as untrustworthy to the RLSH community. But I took a chance, putting my trust in the villains.

In the plot, I meet the Eye as myself, in order to sell them information that I had learned about the Real Life Super Heroes around the world. Ultimately, I end up being a supreme villain in disguise and double-cross the Roaming Eye of Doom. I take their money in exchange for bogus info and beat up the Golden Don, dumping his unconscious body in a bathtub. The short film was very funny, and I found it quite entertaining. Giving me the opportunity to feel like part of their group helped me understand why they tried to keep the community on the right track, and how much fun they had doing it in an original way.

As it stands, the Eye of Doom has found their place in the community, unmasking fake RLSHs, and they are appreciated by credible RLSHs who have proven themselves.

In quiet moments between filming, the Golden Don made a passing comment that stuck with me: "The thing we do is *mock* heroes by being evil. The concept of evil is debatably philosophical. Some people in history, that most would classify as pure evil, probably thought they were actually doing the right thing." I found his thought provoking, yet genuine.

Perhaps actor Tom Hiddleston put it more succinctly: "Every villain is a hero in his own mind."

CONCLUSION

After spending four years interviewing American serial killers, studying psychology, reading about murders and sexual assaults, cruelty and violence, I wanted to dive into a subject that was light, easy, and uncomplicated. My time with RLSHs was anything but; however, I ended my time in the community feeling inspired. I thought of how many RLSHs had turned difficult upbringings and hardships into positives. How many of these superheroes could have taken different, destructive paths? I only encountered four RLSHs whom I would consider unbalanced and potentially unstable, but they are not taken seriously by the rest of the community. They are notorious for their embarrassing actions and scandalous behaviour.

That said, even the best superheroes' motivations may come from psychological issues, but I only approached the ones I considered the real heroes — not the posers, not the trolls, not the attention seekers (well ... at least, not the ones who *just* did that). I wanted to focus on people with good hearts who want to save the world their own way.

In fact, one of my former professors, Stéphane Leclerc, teaches about science fiction in movies. Professor Leclerc has studied psychoanalysis and psychology, and is a specialist in pop culture and cinematography. He also studied semiotics at the doctoral level. In his sci-fi course, he concentrates his superhero lessons on Spider-Man and Batman. He studied the foundations of the human personality and the role of defence mechanisms, like protection and overcompensation.

One day, Stéphane explained the fictional superhero psychology to me:

> The movie *Spider-Man*, from Sam Raimi, was a story about the identity quest for a young teenager in the middle of maturation and searching autonomy. The movie starts with "Who am I?" and ends with "I am Spider-Man." During the steps of the construction of his identity search, Peter Parker is confronted with rejection (especially at the beginning of the movie): he has pimples, he is a nerd, he is short, he was the laughing stock of all. Additionally, he desired Mary Jane, but could not attract even a look from her.
>
> Once he gets bitten by the spider, everything changes. He becomes stronger and wants to accomplish what he was previously deprived of: during one of the sequences, he wants to make money during a wrestling match to buy a car because he thinks that's what attracts women (thus will please Mary Jane). In the comic book, it's different, as he goes to the wrestling match to gain money to help his aunt and uncle. Yet, in the movie, he does it for himself and that will lead to serious consequences. The wrestling promoter refuses to pay him, but at the same time the promoter is robbed by a crook and Peter doesn't intervene. A few moments later, his uncle is killed by the same crook that Peter had ignored a few minutes ago.
>
> From this story, we can see how Peter is confronted with the absurdities of life, which is a reflection of the chaotic post-modern world we all live in (theory of J.P. Sartre and existentialists). In fact, there are many moments in our lives that are absurd, on which we can't always see anything. There are injustices that are absurd:

like seeing his sister being harassed, assaulted at school because of differences....Yet, it's at that moment that an individual can introvert in himself the rejection lived by another person (just like the abused sister, for example) and wants to eventually seek revenge, a compensation for this absurd injustice.

I definitely feel that Spider-Man started with the same mentality as a Real Life Super Hero, especially the ones who fight crime initially as vigilantes. Just like Phoenix Jones in his early days, vigilantes make their own justice. They fight crime by punishing the criminals. I communicated with a RLSH who admitted to severely beating a man who was raping a woman, when the proper thing to do would have been to stop the aggressor and call the police. Even Batman collaborates with police officers to arrest criminals.

Professor Leclerc continued:

But in Spider-Man's case, there is more. Before he died, his uncle told him, "With great power comes great responsibility." That message will be major for Peter, who will have to learn to do better with his new identity characteristics. And that's where the movie connects directly with Aristotle and Plato, concerning the identity construction regarding virtue. Aristotle emphasizes that a virtuous person has to acquire certain qualities: particularly wisdom, courage, temperance and justice. That's what Peter will discover through the story.

At the end of the movie, Mary Jane suggests that they could be together as a couple. Peter refuses: he knows that if he stays with her, it will endanger her life. It takes wisdom to make such an acknowledgement and to step away from someone who has been, our entire life, the subject of our love. It takes courage to disregard our envies and desires for someone, and to decide to abandon this relationship. And it takes courage to tell ourselves that our life is at the service of the population instead of being comfortable at home. It takes temperance to go away from the love we had so desired. And ultimately, what includes all of the other qualities is justice. This last virtue is the most important one because it implies to do what is just and good at all times through our devotion for others.

With great power comes great responsibility. That is why many RLSHs say that when they put the masks on, they are not themselves, per se. Everything they do must be in service to the image of a superhero. But the mask is also there for protection. In Spider-Man's story, just like in real life, Mary Jane and Spider-Man's family are often in trouble because the criminals know who Spider-Man is related to. Mary Jane gets kidnapped, his aunt gets attacked, and so on. There are risks that come with the territory, and they couldn't be more real. So far, RLSHs have been arrested, threatened, and harassed. They've had their tires slashed. They've lost their jobs. But they still want to do good around them.

Leclerc continued:

> This is what builds our identity. Because, in addition to that, you have to believe that there are people weaker than you who need your protection, because they are destitute toward injustice and the absurdity of life. Regarding the superheroes you cover, there is a lot more than that: the courage, the wisdom, the feeling of justice toward the weaker and the poor. It's through their lives and risk of their lives (a certain courage) that they want to help people because they are probably under the impression that what happened to them was unfair and absurd.
>
> On an analytical psychological level, however, I would say there is something impulsive in them: they are confronted with the Thanatos death drive — there is probably a reason why one of the superheroes has that name — while combatting crime, and it gives them an adrenalin rush that makes them live, literally, during the

interventions. They will say they do it out of concern for justice, to do what is good and just, but in fact they do it fundamentally for themselves, as it gives them the feeling of being someone, to exist.

I have to admit that I am guilty, just as the RLSHs are. I had an adrenalin rush when I faced the gunman with Phoenix Jones, and when I was near the two gunmen in Oakland with Motor Mouth. This sensation gave me the drive to patrol even more with the superheroes, rather than being afraid and going back home. It's like facing danger and being willing to suffer the consequences, while feeling powerful. I remember that when the first gunman followed us, I was willing to go talk to him. I thought I might have had a chance to calm him down. Of course, there was a risk of my being shot. If the shot was anywhere non-vital, I was willing to suffer the pain of a gunshot. I was hoping that my bulletproof vest would take care of the rest. Is this really worse than going to war as a journalist?

Stéphane elaborated:

> For the more psychologically problematic, we have to talk about Batman. His problem comes from the guilt he holds in himself because of his parents' deaths, assassination, and for which he feels responsible. I think some of the superheroes you talked about must be confronted with such feelings that they have repressed. For the ex-criminals who now act as heroes, "righters of wrongs," or the one who wants to save the widow and the orphan because he saw his sister being abused — what happened to them? For the ex-criminals, would it be possible that they have guilty consciences because of the harm they did to others? They've introverted that feeling and placed it on actions that are judged good by the society because they feel guilty and responsible for reprehensible actions done in the past? For the one whose sister was abused, would it be possible that he felt helpless when he was younger and that he wants, today, to bring out this feeling, deeply suppressed in himself, of wanting to help and do

good around him? It's about, as we were saying, a feeling
of inferiority that he overcompensates for by taking action
to uphold the law.

Although it appears that superheroes want to save the world, it made
sense to me that they did it for themselves. After all, there must be a
deep motivation to risk their life, their security, or their health (like
the people picking up syringes, for example). In fact, I'm told several
Real Life Super Heroes have received direct threats. There are risks to
the job, but it gives their lives a sense of purpose. It makes them feel
better about themselves.

Leclerc went on:

But there is more. Batman, because of his technology,
wants to be equal to God. He is perfect, powerful, a superman. His sculpted emblem of the persona is important, just like his suit. The emblem appears in the movie
[*Batman* (1989)], in the sky at the end. The journey of the
hero, in that sense, constitutes a mystical ascent, mythical:
he wants to elevate to the level of God. Batman doesn't
advocate God's death, but since God isn't there, he re-
places him. At the end of the story, or when things turn
bad in the estate, when the help is required, you have to
turn toward the sky: his acronym is clearly there. Batman
is found in the sky.

The movie explains the genesis of the hero. It's in-
stalled in the myth: after God, there is Oedipus and culpability. Thus, is it a different psychological element that
animates the character: the culpability that links to his
parents. Look at Batman's pictogram, the Bat signal: a bat,
spread out, oval golden, rimmed with black. It reproduces
the character's aspects. It coincides with its proper representation. It becomes a sign, a symbol, an association
to the reduced image of the man's person. It represents a
generative outline: one gives birth to the other one (just
like Batman's suit or suits of the Real Life Super Heroes

in your book). But with Batman, when we look inside the emblem, just like any image shared in two contrasted adjacent zones, the look is forced to choose between two complementary silhouettes. The result is that we don't see the bat spontaneously, but a gaping yellow metallic mouth. The teeth are round. Thus are they as dangerous? It is rather a child's mouth from a comic book (like Baby Herman). The teeth from the bat aren't there. Is Batman in regression? He has, anyway, a double identity.

Rereading those lines, I could apply this description to the superhero community. Not many of them actually wear colours. Most of their costumes, or gear, as they like to call it, are dark.

It's in that sense that the Real Life Super Heroes carry in themselves this regression that pushes them to act in an impulsive manner disregarding the danger around them. If it's stronger than them, despite the reality of the threat they are confronted with, it's because they are inclined by an uncontrollable and repressed drive that they don't measure the content. All of it originates from conflicts, powerful traumas that they are not in a position to manage and understand. They cast outside of them the feeling under the form of a social legitimization: since some people are in distress, and nobody is there to protect them (they probably question the legal power a certain way, by talking about the inefficiency of the law, thus of God by the other side of the coin), so it's the superhero's role to act....

Yes, I think they might know where their necessity to act comes from: harassment, witnessing brutality, free violence, etc. But the problem is right there: if they are committing these gestures, produce these actions — the ones that represent, accomplish justice — it's because they did not integrate their shadow, their dark side, and they continue the projections (this echoes Carl

Jung). In fact, the problem is that they are not super-heroes. They are humans who cannot make law, to the detriment of the legal justice. They are only humans. Yet movies of superheroes, like *Spider-Man*, should help us build our identity.

But if we have individuals who *play* at being super-heroes, and who have no powers, and who put their lives in danger — it is my opinion that they solve their problem by confronting with *more violence than they lived through when they were younger*. Thus they did not succeed in *curing* their wounds of the past and immortalizing the cycle of what, partially, brought them into the world. They say that they make such or such things because it is bound to their shady past. I say that they would have to consult to channel their anger *somewhere else*. I believe that, unlike Spider-Man who learns according to his evolution, he has to use his powers with *righteousness*, that our real life su-perheroes projecting their anger, their expulsion on the bandits they want to catch. For them, it is a question of one *catharsis*, of *redemption* in front of the negative affect lived in their life, but it contains a danger to consider ourselves invincible, to consider ourselves a superhero. They are not what they would like to be.

The superheroes generally wear a mask. It is, in that sense, the mask/double. It is a question of one *persona*, of the *social identity* that it appears (moreover, we all wear this mask in our everyday lives, as necessary). It is thus through this double (copy) that they sometimes seem to exist, even to exist more by the mask than by their true "I." It is a way to protect their identity (as it is in the case of Batman, among others). But which one? When the mask becomes more important than the reality, there is a substitution. It hides the neurosis at the bottom of one, something that we do not want to see.

I'll give you an example. In *Magnolia*, [directed by] P.T. Anderson, there is a character played by Tom Cruise. He created a select club of men who value the phallic power, the domination of men over women. Yet it is a social mask. Then what hides his real repressed self? As a young person, he had to take care of his dying mother while his father had abandoned him. He saw his mother dying. Older, his impotent rage was projected in his need, strangely, to control women, the *symbolic woman*, which constitutes, represents, the *loss of his childhood and his manliness*.

He avoids the excessive identification, the unhealthy closeness associated with his mother and the disastrous circumstances she faced: the disease. If he identifies too much with her, if he acquires the characteristics of her world too much, it will confirm his loss, her power to destroy him. For him, she painfully represents a burden, the loss of his freedom while very young and in his teen phase. So he abuses women to maintain his *control*, his *detachment*. Furthermore, his loss of manliness resulting from the inability to control the inevitable suffering, the eventual death of his mother, leads him to identify literally and negatively with what he misses: an *image of powerful manliness*.

I believe that there is a little of it in the Real Life Super Heroes. They have lived in weakness and powerlessness (seen victims assaulted, been assaulted themselves, etc.) that their "I" narcissist, building their identity, could not unconsciously accept. Their "real me" rejects their "inept me" recalling the trauma, and they build themselves new identities (masks) that they believe can fill the lack of origin: the weakness, the loss, the powerlessness, the impossibility to act, etc. The mask, the superhero suit, is always what hides our weaknesses. It is the cover that hides our shadows and that we do not especially want to see in ourselves. The neurotic is one who is afraid of his shade....

Personally, I am surprised by the *innocence* of their gesture. They are not aware enough of the consequences of their actions (like Spider-Man, before taking the measure of his power and what comes with it). Who says that one of these days a criminal is not going to give a real lesson to this guy?

That said, I have spoken with many RLSHs about their awareness of the potential risks. The answers are always the same: either, "I can get killed by crossing the street" or something like, "I'd rather die while protecting people." So most Real Life Super Heroes are fully aware of the consequences. Aren't they?

Whether we agree or disagree with them, the fact remains that the good Real Life Super Heroes are willing to give their lives to make the world a better place.

In Canada, my country, the level of violence is not quite like in the United States. Being a Real Life Super Hero is less risky there, thus less of a thrill. For that reason, some RLSHs started to patrol with their gear, but while many guarded the streets for a while, many others quit after a short period of time. I was disappointed when I went to Quebec City to meet with two members of a four-person team, only to find out that they had quit after only a few patrols. In Montreal, however, RLSHs Noxx and LightStep have continued patrolling the streets and giving food to the homeless. Polarman in Iqaluit, Nunavut, has been extremely active and defends and teaches people about bullying in schools. Crimson Canuck, in Windsor, Ontario, patrolled the streets for a while. After over a year of seeing the harassment online, however, he decided to quit the RLSH movement, but he continues his work as an ordinary citizen. Ottawa, Toronto, and many other cities have "Maple Leaf" superheroes.

⚡

In all my years of journalism, this book has been one of my hardest assignments. I wrote it, rewrote it, and finally rewrote it again. I kept asking myself: "What can I say? What secrets should I keep?" I had to be careful about not giving too many details. It's not my goal to "out" anybody and, in doing so, cause potential harm. On the other hand, if they gave me the green light, I wrote as much as I could. The more I could reveal, the more I could show the positive and negative aspects of this unusual community, populated as it is with some people who dedicate their lives to others. Yet if I were to judge how many genuine and hardworking people there are in the community, I would say that the real and honest "heroes" probably represent only about 5 percent of the total. So how much of the "unreal heroes" should I write about? How much negativity should I unveil? It was sometimes overwhelming to pursue a positive line, only to later feel the need to comment on some of the wackier elements of this world. I have tried to be even-handed. There's no escaping the fact that it takes a certain amount of eccentricity to get dressed up and patrol the streets. And I had to point out some of the downright juvenile behaviour I observed in the online community. I also met generous and kind-hearted people who would trade their lives for someone else's happiness. Yet there were others who seemed to be simply looking for attention, like the cries for help of so many real-world bullies. However, I am thankful to have crossed the paths of some inspiring people, many of whom have found the power to turn their lives around.

⚡

The information provided to me for this book has been verified to the best of my ability. However, some of the content relayed during the interviews could not be verified. That's probably always going to be the case when dealing with people with secret identities.

Over the course of my research and writing, I also noticed the groups of Real Life Super Villains and Real Life Super Heroes changing. Older ones left … new ones joined. … A disagreement formed in the Eye of Doom as the Golden Don did not agree with the team's increasingly hard approach. As a result, he chose to end his role as a villain. Further conflict followed in the community when the Eye tried to merge with the Initiative. After all, what good are villains if they're directly allied to heroes?

On the other hand, other villains, such as Lord Malignance, remain involved, continuing to shine a light on the activities of RLSHs. Even after so many years in the community, he's kept his integrity and continues to fight for what he believes is right. Tamerlane is also very active and routinely films himself "on patrol." His patrols are often focused on pestering people whom he sees as being aligned with fascism.

As for Phoenix Jones, he will always be hated by some and loved by others, but while many heroes have quit, he is one of the superheroes who continues to patrol. He makes mistakes, learns, and adjusts his actions. One important change he made is that he no longer criticizes heroes who "only" feed the homeless.

Since my time with PJ in Seattle, he has kicked the Mantis off his team. The Mantis — the one who had the Rain City Superhero Movement logo tattooed on his arm — pawned a bulletproof vest that PJ had given him. Then he lied about it. It was enough of a breach of trust that PJ simply did not want to work with the Mantis any longer.

Purple Reign has unmasked herself, although she hesitated for a long time. But she said she had to, in order to show that victims of domestic violence need not hide in the shadows. She figured that having a mask on her face was a little contradictory. Purple continues to dedicate her time to helping both men and women who are victims of domestic violence. She raises funds and strives to be a great role model for victims. Although she still participates in some activities, she hasn't been visible in the superhero community in a while.

Thanatos is another who hasn't been seen in a long time. Because of his age, many RLSHs wonder if he decided to retire.

Sadly, Rouroni, one of the members of the Xtreme Justice League, died in a fatal car accident. He is remembered as one of the most dedicated RLSHs out there. Rest in peace, Rouroni.

Many of the Initiative members no longer wear masks. They say that they and their superhero personas have become the same person. Other people in the community believe it is because they personally want the gratification.

On the other hand, people like Rock N Roll and NightBug continue their own training. On top of their training in many martial arts, first aid, and firearms use, they have both completed the Citizen Police Academy Training. They are also teaching self-defence courses to women at no charge, and they raised funds for four different children who needed medical help.

Rock N Roll posted a message on Facebook that I hope many teens and young adults will read:

Years ago, I was in an abusive relationship, broke, unhealthy from over-eating, homophobic, damning anyone who didn't share my religious beliefs, and just plain unhappy. One day I decided to take my head out of my ass, get off my butt, quit being a victim, and make my life better for myself.

I wouldn't change places with anyone because I've worked so hard to be this happy. And it all started when I understood that life is too precious to waste on wishing things were better, and on condemning that which we don't understand. Every day I work on providing my own happiness and spreading it around. It's a circle of positivity and it keeps coming back to me.

What are you working on?

Indeed, life can be difficult. Nonetheless, people like Rock N Roll or Purple Reign show that ordinary people can make positive changes in their own lives and help others to achieve the same.

Discovering this world gave me hope. Hope that more people will care about each other and care about strangers, even if their initial motivation is to tend to their own psychological baggage. It gave me hope that people with a troubled past can also turn their lives around if they really want to.

$$\large \lightning$$

After about two years of research, interviews, and then patrols, I wrote the first draft of the book. I'd already moved on to writing other stories, but I kept an eye on the RLSH community. I saw a lot of positivity, but I also witnessed a lot of negativity. The negativity was overwhelming at times, but I found myself staying in touch with a small number of the heroes that I had met. A very small number of them have become friends.

With the writing of this book behind me, I wanted to reunite with the superheroes one last time. As the Golden Don had retired from the community, we made an impromptu road trip to help at the HOPE event in San Diego. There, we had the chance to meet with over 50 RLSHs, including some I had interviewed but never had the chance to meet in person, such as Geist, DC's Guardian, and others I had patrolled with, such as Rock N Roll, NightBug, Cheshire Cat, Mr. Xtreme, Grim, and Urban Avenger. Rouroni's mother was also at the event.

That day hundreds of bags of food and other practical items were distributed to the poor. To celebrate after the hard day of work, many of us went out to a karaoke place and had lots of fun singing our guts out!

As you can imagine, most RLSHs share similar interests and travel to meet each other for different projects: defending the defenceless, feeding the hungry, teaching self-defence, spreading love around them. So it's not surprising that among the estimated six hundred active people, several serious relationships have formed in the world of RSLHs and RLSVs. After all, something common had brought them all together. Kaptain Blackheart and the Baroness got married, as well as at least two other couples I know of. I wish them and everyone else a joyful life filled with love.

As for me, my life was changed forever. After I had finished with this book, I maintained contact with a few superheroes. I also had to pursue a personal quest. I met with the Golden Don again. I could finally be myself, in a non-working mode. The person behind the Golden Don turned out to be an amazing man. He became my confidant, someone I could trust, a person who inspired me. We spent a lot of time together and our relationship developed.

Sometime later …

I married the Golden Don.

ACKNOWLEDGEMENTS

A huge thank you to all my heroes. They contributed their time to help me complete this book: Robert Livingston, Richard Grove, Judy Grove, Scott Grove, Sage Michael, Yaiza Magdalena, Ashley Sanchez, Christina Beaudette Hindley, Simon Normand, Bianca Veilleux, Anne-Marie Traore, Lynn Azanbou, Steven Casper, Lee Winkleman, Linda Armstrong, Scott Fraser, Joseph Jones, Françoise Jacob, Benoît Lessard, Nathalie Vandevelve, Shawn Sirois, Roxanne Laferrière, Bastien Blondin, Noëlle Charpentier, Jean-François Blouin, Anouk Hagemann, Cindy Fauchon, Geneviève Tellier, Pascal Lapointe, Stéphane Leclerc, Peter Tangen, Ryan McNamee, and Terri Duvalis Alder.

Also, a colossal thank you to all the Real Life Super Heroes and Real Life Super Villains who opened up to me and welcomed me into their lives.